FROM WILDERNESS
TO GLORY

Access free digital resources at
www.wjkbooks.com/LentForEveryone
that include a group study guide, images for use
during worship or group study and resources
to promote your outreach.

FROM WILDERNESS TO GLORY

Lent and Easter for Everyone

N. T. Wright

WESTMINSTER
JOHN KNOX PRESS
LOUISVILLE · KENTUCKY

Original edition published in English under the title *Lent and Easter for Everyone: From Wilderness to Glory* by SPCK Publishing, a wholly owned subsidiary of The Society for Promoting Christian Knowledge, London, England, UK. This edition copyright © 2023 SPCK Publishing.

Published in the United States of America in 2025
by Westminster John Knox Press,
100 Witherspoon Street, Louisville, KY 40202

25 26 27 28 29 30 31 32 33 34—10 9 8 7 6 5 4 3 2

Scripture quotations from the New Testament are the author's own translation.

Scripture quotations from the Old Testament are taken from the New Revised Standard Version of the Bible, Anglicized Edition, copyright © 1989, 1995 by the Division of Christian Education of the National Council of the Churches of Christ in the USA. Used by permission. All rights reserved.

Cover design by designpointinc.com

Library of Congress Cataloging-in-Publication Data

Names: Wright, N. T. (Nicholas Thomas) author.
Title: From wilderness to glory : Lent and Easter for everyone / N.T. Wright.
Description: First US edition. | Louisville, Kentucky : Westminster John Knox Press, 2025. | "First published in Great Britain in 2023 by SPCK." | Summary: "Compiles passages from Wright's New Testament for Everyone series to provide a daily devotional for the Lent and Easter season. Each day includes his translation of a Scripture passage, words of reflection, and questions for reflection or discussion"-- Provided by publisher.
Identifiers: LCCN 2024042362 (print) | LCCN 2024042363 (ebook) | ISBN 9780664268862 (paperback) | ISBN 9781646984107 (ebook)
Subjects: LCSH: Lent--Prayers and devotions. | Holy Week--Prayers and devotions. | Easter--Prayers and devotions.
Classification: LCC BV85 .W7133 2025 (print) | LCC BV85 (ebook) | DDC 242/.34--dc23/eng/20241101
LC record available at https://lccn.loc.gov/2024042362
LC ebook record available at https://lccn.loc.gov/2024042363

Most Westminster John Knox Press books are available at special quantity discounts when purchased in bulk by corporations, organizations and special-interest groups. For more information, please e-mail SpecialSales@wjkbooks.com.

Contents

Contents

Contents

Introduction

The early Christians were *different*. Different from the Greeks and Romans, the Egyptians and Syrians in whose world they lived, their next-door neighbours and, often enough, their extended families. Different, too, though in a different way, from the Jewish families and communities to whom, again, many Jesus-followers would be related. The early Christians were marked out in many ways, but one of the most distinctive was something they *did* every year. The first solid evidence for this comes from about three hundred years after the time of Jesus, but this clearly reflects an already established practice.

Something they did; or, perhaps we should say, something they didn't do. They kept what we now call 'Lent': a time to abstain, to fast, to clear the mental, spiritual and physical horizon in order to focus on prayer, penitence, holiness and hope in the days and weeks before Easter.

Lent didn't stand alone. Many Christians today, if they keep 'Lent' at all, follow it with only a single day of Easter celebration. But the early Christians celebrated Easter as a prolonged festival, running for forty days until the commemoration of Jesus' Ascension. The present book, ending with a whole week of Easter reflections, is pointing towards that larger reality.

Why did they do all this? What did it mean for them? And what might it mean for us to follow the same kind of discipline?

Perhaps the most important thing they were doing was to remind themselves, in the weeks either side of Easter, that world history divides into two: the time before Jesus' death and resurrection, and the time afterwards. New creation has been launched in the midst of the old. This huge claim challenges the way most of the world thought, and thinks. To get it into our hearts, minds and lives, we adopt this ancient practice of a time of lament followed by a time of celebration. Though we do indeed now live in the ongoing 'Easter season' – ever since God's new creation was launched with Jesus' resurrection, and energized with the fresh gift of his spirit – we can never simply take it for granted. It has to become real, and fresh, in our own lives. New creation requires renewed humans at its heart. Keeping Lent and Easter is an excellent way of maintaining that fresh reality.

The sharp distinction between Lent and Easter reminds us of a double truth many Christians today easily forget.

First, the importance of *lament*. It's easy, when carried away with the joy of the gospel, to ignore the fact that the world is still in a mess; that the church is often muddled and sinful; that we ourselves still fail miserably in our love for God and for one another. At this point some-one might say 'Oh, that sounds so gloomy! Surely God wants us to be cheerful?' But, actually, the gift of lament points to the true joy of the gospel. Being a Christian doesn't mean pretending that everything is 'all right really' when actually it isn't. To lament is to recognize that things still *are* out of joint, and that we can and should bring our puzzled sorrow and frustration into God's presence. God's gift of lament (following the Jesus who, according to Isaiah 53.3, was 'a man of sorrows and acquainted with infirmity') is the way we join in with God's own sorrow at the continuing tragedy of his world.

Second, though, the importance of genuine *celebration*. Keeping the season of Easter isn't whistling in the dark. It is opening our eyes to the light – and, in astonished gratitude, determining day by day to live in that light. Once we get Lent right – once we learn to lament properly, with our bodies as well as our minds and hearts – we can then praise God for Jesus' death and resurrection, and for the new creation into which we have been brought, without any danger of making it sound cheap or trivial.

The church has always known, intuitively even, that the best way for us to be shaped into the people God wants us to be – the people whose difference from the world around is vital to our witness – is to think and pray slowly and carefully through the stories of Jesus' life, death and resurrection. This book is designed to help you to do just that. May God be with you in this journey.

Tom Wright
Wycliffe Hall, Oxford

Prologue
Jesus in the wilderness

Ash Wednesday

Jesus' baptism: Mark 1.9–13

[9]This is how it happened. Around that time, Jesus came from Nazareth in Galilee, and was baptized by John in the river Jordan. [10]That very moment, as he was coming out of the water, he saw the heavens open, and the spirit coming down like a dove onto him. [11]Then there came a voice out of the heavens: 'You are my son! You are the one I love! You make me very glad.'

[12]All at once the spirit pushed him out into the desert. [13]He was in the desert forty days, and the satan tested him there. He was with the wild beasts, and angels waited on him.

A famous movie-maker had a huge legal wrangle with his long-time mentor and guide. The younger man simply couldn't handle criticism, and ended up rejecting the person who had helped him so much. When it was all over, a close friend summed up the real problem. 'It was all about an ungenerous father,' he explained, 'and a son looking for affirmation and love.' It happens all the time, in families, businesses, all over. Many children grow up in our world who have never had a father say to them (either in words, in looks, or in hugs), 'You are my dear child', let alone, 'I'm pleased with you.' In the Western world, even those fathers who think this in their hearts are often too tongue-tied or embarrassed to tell their children how delighted they are with them. Many, alas, go by the completely opposite route: angry voices, bitter rejection, the slamming of doors.

The whole Christian gospel could be summed up in this point: that when the living God looks at us, at every baptized and believing Christian, he says to us what he said to Jesus on that day. He sees us, not as we are in ourselves, but as we are in Jesus Christ. It sometimes seems impossible, especially to people who have never had this kind of support from their earthly parents, but it's true: God looks at us, and says, 'You are my dear, dear child; I'm delighted with you.'

How does this come about? It will take the whole story, particularly Jesus' death and resurrection, to explain. But this is what the Christian gospel is all about.

It is true for one simple but very profound reason: Jesus is the Messiah, and the Messiah represents his people. What is true of him is true of them. The word 'Messiah' means 'the anointed one'; and this story tells how Jesus was anointed with the holy spirit, marked out as God's son. The Messiah is called 'God's son' in a few biblical passages, including the one that the heavenly voice seems to be echoing here (Psalm 2.7). Though the early Christians realized quite quickly that Jesus was God's son in an even deeper sense, they clung on to his messiahship for dear life. It was because Jesus was and is Messiah that God said to them, as he does to us today, what he said to Jesus at his baptism. And without that word from God all we often hear, in our mind's ear, is doors being slammed.

Mark tells the story in quite solemn language, echoing the Old Testament: 'This is how it happened'; 'he saw the heavens open'. If we go back to the biblical roots we will realize what 'seeing heavens opened' means. It doesn't mean that Jesus saw a little door ajar miles up in the sky. 'Heaven' in the Bible often means God's dimension behind ordinary reality. It's more as though an invisible curtain, right in front of us, was suddenly pulled back, so that instead of the trees and flowers and buildings, or in Jesus' case the river, the sandy desert and the crowds, we are standing in the presence of a different reality altogether.

A good deal of Christian faith is a matter of learning to live by this different reality even when we can't see it. Sometimes, at decisive and climactic moments, the curtain is drawn back and we see, or hear, what's really going on; but most of the time we walk by faith, not by sight. One of the things Mark is saying to us is that when we look at the whole life of Jesus that's how we are to understand it. Look at this story, he says, look at this life, and learn to see and hear in it the heavenly vision, the heavenly voice. Learn to hear these words addressed to yourself. Let them change you, mould you, make you somebody new, the person God wants you to be. Discover in this story the normally hidden heavenly dimension of God's world.

Any early Christian reading this passage would also, of course, believe that their own baptism into Jesus the Messiah was the moment when, for them, the curtain had been drawn back and these words had been spoken to them. We need to find ways, in today's church, of bringing this to life with our own practice of baptism and teaching about it.

When we do this, we will be equipped, as Jesus was, to be sent out into the desert. Jesus is acting out the great drama of Israel's Exodus from Egypt, Israel's journey through the wilderness into the promised land. The road Jesus must tread, precisely because he is God's dear son, is the road that leads through the dry and dusty paths, through temptation and apparent failure. So it will be for us as well. If we start the journey imagining that our God is a bully, an angry threatening parent ready to yell at us, slam the door on us, or kick us out into the street because we haven't quite made the grade, we will fail at the first whisper of temptation. But if we remember the voice that spoke those powerful words of love we will find the way through.

Mark tells us that Jesus was 'with the wild beasts'. He doesn't say whether they're threatening, or whether this is a sign of new creation (with Jesus as the second Adam in a new garden of Eden?) or maybe both. But the angels were there, too. They were not to keep Jesus from being tested by satan, just as finally they would not keep him from Calvary itself, but to assure him that his beloved Father was watching over him, was there with him, was loving him, acting through him, pouring out his spirit all the time in and through him. Jesus went the way that all his people must go; and he could do it because he had heard the words of love, the words of life.

For reflection or discussion

- Imagine God saying these words to you that he said to Jesus at his baptism: 'You are my dear, dear child; I'm delighted with you.' Try reading that sentence slowly, with your own name at the start, and reflect on God saying that to you, both at your baptism and every day since.

- In what ways can you learn to live by God's heavenly reality even though you can't see it? What role does faith play in experiencing this hidden dimension of God's world?

Thursday

Temptation in the wilderness 1: Matthew 4.1–11

[1]Jesus was led out into the wilderness by the spirit to be tested by the devil. [2]He fasted for forty days and forty nights, and at the end of it was famished. [3]Then the tempter approached him.

'If you really are God's son,' he said, 'tell these stones to become bread!'

[4]'The Bible says', replied Jesus, 'that it takes more than bread to keep you alive. You actually live on every word that comes out of God's mouth.'

[5]Then the devil took him off to the holy city, and stood him on a pinnacle of the Temple.

[6]'If you really are God's son,' he said, 'throw yourself down. The Bible does say, after all, that "God will give his angels a

4

command about you"; and "they will carry you in their hands, so that you won't hurt your foot against a stone."'

⁷'But the Bible also says', replied Jesus, 'that you mustn't put the Lord your God to the test!'

⁸Then the devil took him off again, this time to a very high mountain. There he showed him all the magnificent kingdoms of the world.

⁹'I'll give the whole lot to you,' he said, 'if you will fall down and worship me.'

¹⁰'Get out of it, satan!' replied Jesus. 'The Bible says, "Worship the Lord your God, and serve him alone!"'

¹¹Then the devil left him, and angels came and looked after him.

One early Christian writer tells us that Jesus was tempted like other humans in every possible way (Hebrews 4.15). We shouldn't be surprised, then, that after his great moment of vision, when his sense of God's calling and love was so dramatically confirmed at his baptism, he had to face the whispering voices and recognize them for what they were. These suggestions are all ways of distorting the true vocation: the vocation to be a truly human being, to be God's person, to be a servant to the world and to other people. Jesus must face these temptations now, and win at least an initial victory over them. If he doesn't, they will meet him suddenly, in the middle of his work, and they may overwhelm him.

The first two temptations play on the very strength he has just received. 'You are my son, my beloved one!' God had said to him. Very well, whispers the demonic voice; if you really are God's son, surely he can't want you to go hungry when you have the power to get food for yourself? Surely you want people to see who you are? Why not do something really spectacular? And then, dropping the apparent logic, the enemy comes out boldly: forget your heavenly father. Just worship me and I'll give you power, greatness like no one else ever had.

Jesus sees through the trap. He answers, each time, with the Bible and with God. He is committed to living off God's word; to trusting God completely, without setting up trick tests to put God on the spot. He is committed to loving and serving God alone. The flesh may scream for satisfaction; the world may beckon seductively; the devil himself may offer undreamed-of power; but Israel's loving God, the one Jesus knew as father, offered the reality of what it meant to be human, to be a true Israelite, to be Messiah.

The biblical texts Jesus used as his key weapons help us to see how this remarkable story fits into Matthew's gospel at this point. They are all taken from the story of Israel in the wilderness. Jesus had come through the waters of baptism, like Israel crossing the Red Sea. He now had to face, in forty days and nights, the equivalent of Israel's forty years in the desert. But, where Israel failed again and again, Jesus succeeded. Here at last is a true Israelite, Matthew is saying. He has come to do what God always wanted Israel to do – to bring light to the world (see verse 16).

Behind that again is the even deeper story of Adam and Eve in the garden. A single command; a single temptation; a single, devastating, result. Jesus kept his eyes on his father, and so launched the mission to undo the age-old effects of human rebellion. He would meet the tempter again in various guises: protesting to him, through his closest associate, that he should change his mind about going to the cross (16.23); mocking him, through the priests and bystanders, as he hung on the cross (27.39–43, again with the words 'if you are God's son'). This is no accident. When Jesus refused to go the way of the tempter he was embracing the way of the cross. The enticing whispers that echoed around his head were designed to distract him from his central vocation, the road to which his baptism had committed him, the path of servanthood that would lead to suffering and death. They were meant to stop him from carrying out God's calling, to redeem Israel and the world.

The temptations we all face, day by day and at critical moments of decision and vocation in our lives, may be very different from those of Jesus, but they have exactly the same point. They are not simply trying to entice us into committing this or that sin. They are trying to distract us, to turn us aside, from the path of servanthood to which our baptism has commissioned us. God has a costly but wonderfully glorious vocation for each one of us. The enemy will do everything possible to distract us and thwart God's purpose. If we have heard God's voice welcoming us as his children, we will also hear the whispered suggestions of the enemy.

But, as God's children, we are entitled to use the same defence as the son of God himself. Store scripture in your heart, and know how to use it. Keep your eyes on God, and trust him for everything. Remember your calling, to bring God's light into the world. And say a firm 'no' to the voices that lure you back into the darkness.

For reflection or discussion

- In facing temptation, Jesus relies on his relationship with God, and on God's words recorded in scripture. How can you cultivate a similar reliance on God's word and a deep trust in him in the face of your own temptations and challenges?
- The temptations Jesus faced were an attempt to distract him from his central vocation and the path of servanthood. How do the temptations you encounter in your life attempt to distract you from your own calling and purpose as a follower of Jesus? How can you discern and resist these distractions to stay true to your calling?

Friday

Temptation in the wilderness 2: Luke 4.1–13

[1]Jesus returned from the Jordan, filled with the spirit. The spirit took him off into the wilderness [2]for forty days, to be tested by the devil. He ate nothing during that time, and at the end of it he was hungry.

³'If you are God's son,' said the devil, 'tell this stone to become a loaf of bread.'

⁴'It is written,' replied Jesus, '"It isn't only bread that keeps you alive."'

⁵The devil then took him up and showed him, in an instant, all the kingdoms of the world.

⁶'I will give you authority over all of this,' said the devil, 'and all the prestige that goes with it. It's been given to me, you see, and I give it to anyone I like. ⁷So it can all be yours . . . if you will just worship me.'

⁸'It is written,' replied Jesus, '"The Lord your God is the one you must worship; he is the only one you must serve."'

⁹Then the devil took him to Jerusalem, and stood him on a pinnacle of the Temple.

'If you are God's son,' he said, 'throw yourself down from here; ¹⁰it's written, after all, that "He will give his angels a command about you, to look after you"; ¹¹and "They will carry you in their hands, so that you won't hit your foot against a stone."'

¹²'It has been said,' replied Jesus, '"You mustn't put the Lord your God to the test."'

¹³When the devil had finished each temptation, he left him until another opportunity.

Jesus was not Superman. Many today, including some devout Christians, see him as a kind of Christian version of the movie character, able to do whatever he wanted, to 'zap' reality into any shape he liked. In the movies, Superman looks like an ordinary human being, but really he isn't. Underneath the disguise he is all-powerful, a kind of computer-age super-magician. That's not the picture of Jesus we get in the New Testament.

Luke has just reminded us of Jesus' membership in the family of Adam. If there had been any doubt about his being really human,

Luke underlines his sharing of our flesh and blood in this vivid scene of temptation. If Jesus is the descendant of Adam, he must now face not only what Adam faced but the powers that had been unleashed through human rebellion and sin. Long years of habitual rebellion against the creator God had brought about a situation in which the world, the flesh and the devil had become used to twisting human beings into whatever shape they wanted.

In particular, after his baptism, Jesus faced the double question: what did it mean to be God's son in this special, unique way? And what sort of messiahship was he to pursue? There had, after all, been many royal movements in his time, not only the well-known house of Herod but also other lesser-known figures whom we meet in the historian Josephus. Characters like Simon (not one of the Simons we know in the Bible) and Athronges gathered followers and were hailed as kings, only to be cut down by Roman or Herodian troops. There were would-be prophets who promised their followers signs from heaven, great miracles to show God's saving power. They too didn't last long. What was Jesus to do?

The three temptations can be read as possible answers to this question. The story does not envisage Jesus engaged in conversation with a visible figure to whom he could talk as one to another; the devil's voice appears as a string of natural ideas in his own head. They are plausible, attractive, and make, as we would say, a lot of sense. God can't want his beloved son to be famished with hunger, can he? If God wants Jesus to become sovereign over the world (that, after all, is what Gabriel had told Mary), then why not go for it in one easy stride? If Jesus is Israel's Messiah, why not prove it by spectacular displays of power?

If there are in this story echoes of Adam and Eve in the garden, with the serpent whispering plausible lies about God, his purposes and his commands, there are also echoes of Israel in the wilderness. Israel came out of Egypt through the Red Sea, with God declaring that Israel was his son, his firstborn. There then followed the forty-year wandering in the wilderness, where Israel grumbled for bread, flirted disastrously with idolatry, and put God continually to the test. Now Jesus, coming through the waters of baptism as God's unique son, the one through whom Israel's destiny was to be fulfilled, faces the question: how is he to be Israel's representative, her rightful king? How can he deliver Israel, and thereby the world, from the grip of the enemy? How can he bring about the real liberation, not just from Rome and other political foes, but from the archenemy, the devil himself?

The answer is that he must begin by defeating him at the most personal and intimate level. Christian leaders today sometimes make the mistake of thinking that as long as they are pursuing the right aims in their public life, what they do in private doesn't matter so much. That is a typical lie whispered by the same voice that Jesus heard in the desert. If God is working by his spirit through a person, that person's own life will be increasingly formed by that spirit, through testing at every level. If Jesus could not win the victory there, there was little point carrying on.

Jesus responds to the devil, not by attempting to argue (arguing with temptation is often a way of playing with the idea until it becomes too attractive to resist), but by quoting scripture. The passages he draws on come from the story of Israel in the wilderness: he is going to succeed where Israel failed. Physical needs and wants are important, but loyalty to God is more important still. Jesus is indeed to become the world's true lord, but the path to that status, and the mode of it when it arrives, is humble service, not a devilish seeking after status and power. Trust in God doesn't mean acting stupidly to force God into doing a spectacular rescue. The power that Jesus already has, which he will shortly display in healings in particular, is to be used for restoring others to life and strength, not for cheap stunts. His status as God's son commits him, not to showy prestige, but to the strange path of humility, service and finally death. The enemy will return to test this resolve again. For the moment, an initial victory is won, and Jesus can begin his public career knowing that though struggles lie ahead the foe has been beaten on the first field that really matters.

We are unlikely to be tempted in exactly the same way as Jesus was, but every Christian will be tested at the points which matter most in her or his life and vocation. It is a central part of Christian vocation to learn to recognize the voices that whisper attractive lies, to distinguish them from the voice of God, and to use the simple but direct weapons provided in scripture to rebut the lies with truth.

The Christian discipline of fighting temptation is not about self-hatred, or rejecting parts of our God-given humanity. It is about celebrating God's gift of full humanity and, like someone learning a musical instrument, discovering how to tune it and play it to its best possibility. At the heart of our resistance to temptation is love and loyalty to the God who has already called us his beloved children in Christ, and who holds out before us the calling to follow him in the path which leads to the true glory. In that glory lies the true happiness, the true fulfilment, which neither world, nor flesh, nor devil can begin to imitate.

For reflection or discussion

- In facing temptation, Jesus rejects the path of cheap and easy stunts or showy prestige. How can you learn to trust in God's timing and guidance, resisting the temptation to manipulate situations for your own gain or to seek instant gratification?
- The passage highlights the importance of recognizing the voices that whisper attractive lies and distinguishing them from the voice of God. How can we develop discernment and wisdom in identifying and resisting the deceptive messages that surround us in our culture?

Saturday

The snake and the love of God: John 3.1–3, 14–21

[1]There was a man of the Pharisees called Nicodemus, a ruler of the Judaeans. [2]He came to Jesus by night.

'Rabbi,' he said to him. 'We know that you're a teacher who's come from God. . . '

[3]'Let me tell you the solemn truth,' replied Jesus. . .

[14]'Just as Moses lifted up the snake in the desert, in the same way the son of man must be lifted up, [15]so that everyone who believes in him may share in the life of God's new age. [16]This, you see, is how much God loved the world: enough to give his only, special son, so that everyone who believes in him should not be lost but should share in the life of God's new age. [17]After all, God didn't send the son into the world to condemn the world, but so that the world could be saved by him.

[18]'Anyone who believes in him is not condemned. But anyone who doesn't believe is condemned already, because they didn't believe in the name of God's only, special son. [19]And this is the condemnation: that light has come into the world, and people loved darkness rather than light, because what they were doing was evil. [20]For everyone who does evil hates the light; people like that don't come to the light, in case their deeds get shown up and reproved. [21]But people who do the truth come to the light, so that it can become clear that what they have done has been done in God.'

'And mind you watch out for snakes!'

My wife gave me a final warning before I set off into the hills. The footpaths had been closed for several months because of a widespread and infectious animal disease. Many creatures that normally kept away from regular footpaths had, apparently, spent the spring enjoying a new-found freedom. We don't have many dangerous snakes in the British Isles, but the viper is dangerous enough. And, to be honest, I didn't know exactly what I would do if I met one.

Fortunately, I didn't see one on the walk. But it sent my mind back to the way in which the symbol of the snake has been used in many cultures over many thousands of years. From the snake in the Garden of Eden to the serpent Ananta in some branches of Hinduism, to the mythic serpent-ancestor of the Aztecs and the 'old god of nature' in parts of Africa to this day; from poetry to art and medicine, not least psychoanalysis; the figure of the serpent or snake has haunted human imagination from time immemorial.

In many cultures, the serpent is seen as positive and power-ful, though dangerous. In many others, not least in some parts of the Jewish and Christian traditions, the serpent is seen as a strong negative force, symbolizing the evil in the world and in all of us. The question of what to do about the serpent is a way of asking the question of what to do about evil – or what different cultures have designated as evil.

The present passage gives a clear and confident answer, which has itself been powerful in subsequent thought and culture. Verse 14 looks back to the incident described in Numbers 21.5–8. During their wandering in the wilderness, the Israelites grumbled against Moses, and were punished by poisonous snakes invading the camp, killing many of them. God gave Moses the remedy: he was to make a ser-pent out of bronze, put it on a pole and hold it up for people to look at. Anyone who looked at the serpent on the pole would live. The serpent entwined around the pole, a symbol which appears in other cultures too, remains to this day as a sign of healing, used by various medical organizations.

The bronze serpent was thereafter stored in the Tabernacle as a sacred object, until, much later, King Hezekiah discovered that the people were worshipping it, and broke it to pieces (2 Kings 18.4). In the time of Jesus, one Jewish writer found it necessary to emphasize that it wasn't the bronze serpent itself that had saved the Israelites, but the saving power of God (Wisdom of Solomon 16.7). All this shows the strange power of the symbol, and highlights even more the importance of verse 14 for understanding what Jesus had come to do.

This, in fact, is the only place in the New Testament where the bronze serpent is referred to. Here it points clearly to the death of Jesus. Moses put the serpent on a pole, and lifted it up so the people could see it; even so, the son of man must be lifted up, so that everyone who believes in him may have eternal life. Humankind as a whole has been smitten with a deadly disease. The only cure is to look at the son of man dying on the cross, and find life through believing in him.

This is very deep and mysterious, but we must ask: how can the crucifixion of Jesus be like putting the snake on a pole? Wasn't the snake the problem, not the solution? Surely John isn't suggesting that Jesus was like the poisonous snakes that had been attacking the people?

No, he isn't. What he is saying, and will continue to say in several ways right up to his account of the crucifixion, is that the evil which was and is in the world, deep-rooted within us all, was somehow allowed to take out its full force on Jesus. When we look at him hanging on the cross, what we are looking at is the result of the evil in which we are all stuck. And we are seeing what God has done about it.

We are seeing, in particular, what God's own love looks like. John refers us back to 1.18, and behind that to 1.1–2, in order to say: when Jesus died on the cross, that was the full and dramatic display of God's own love. It wasn't a messy accident; it wasn't God letting the worst happen to someone else. The cross is at the heart of John's amazing new picture of who God is. He is now to be known as the God who is both father and son, and the son is revealed, 'lifted up', when he dies under the weight of the world's evil. The cross is the ultimate ladder set up between heaven and earth.

But evil isn't then healed, as it were, automatically. Precisely because evil lurks deep within each of us, for healing to take place we must ourselves be involved in the process. This doesn't mean that we just have to try a lot harder to be good. You might as well try to teach a snake to sing. All we can do, just as it was all the Israelites could do, is to look and trust: to look at Jesus, to see in him the full display of God's saving love, and to trust in him.

Here there opens up the great divide, which John describes in terms of darkness and light (see 1.4–5). Believing in Jesus means coming to the light, the light of God's new creation. Not believing means remaining in the darkness. The darkness (and those who embrace it) must be condemned, not because it offends against some arbitrary laws which God made up for the fun of it, and certainly not because it has to do with the material, created world rather than with a supposed 'spiritual' world. It must be condemned because evil is destroying and defacing the present world, and preventing people coming forward into God's new world ('eternal life'; that is, the life of the age to come).

But the point of the whole story is that you don't have to be condemned. You don't have to let the snake kill you. God's action in the crucifixion of Jesus has planted a sign in the middle of history. And the sign says: believe, and live.

For reflection or discussion

- How does the symbol of the bronze snake on a pole in the wilderness relate to the crucifixion of Jesus? In what ways does it reveal God's saving love?
- What role do belief and trust play in the process of healing and salvation?

Week 1
Jesus among the crowds

Monday

Jesus calls the disciples: Matthew 4.18–25

[18]As Jesus was walking beside the sea of Galilee he saw two brothers, Simon (also called Peter) and Andrew his brother. They were fishermen, and were casting nets into the sea. [19]'Follow me!' said Jesus. 'I'll make you fish for people!' [20]Straight away they abandoned their nets and followed him.

[21]He went on further, and saw two other brothers, James the son of Zebedee and John his brother. They were in the boat, mending their nets, with Zebedee their father. He called them. [22]At once they left the boat, and their father, and followed him.

[23]He went on through the whole of Galilee, teaching in their synagogues and proclaiming the good news of the kingdom, healing every disease and every illness among the people.

[24]Word about him went out around the whole of Syria. They brought to him all the people tormented with various kinds of diseases and ailments, demon-possessed people, epileptics, and paralytics, and he healed them. [25]Large crowds followed him from Galilee, the Ten Towns, Jerusalem, Judaea and beyond the Jordan.

If you go to Galilee today they will show you a boat that might have belonged to Andrew and Peter, or perhaps the Zebedee family.

In one of the most remarkable archaeological finds anywhere in the Holy Land (which is full of them), a boat was found sticking out of the mud one summer when the level of the Sea of Galilee dropped dramatically in a period of dry weather. With great care it was lifted clear of the sea bottom, cleaned and preserved. Now, in a special exhibit, millions of visitors can see the sort of boat Jesus' first followers used for fishing. It has been carbon-dated to exactly the period of Jesus' life.

The boat is a vivid reminder of the day-to-day existence of his followers – and of what it cost them to give it all up and follow Jesus. They were, in today's language, small businessmen, working as families not for huge profits but to make enough to live on and have a little over. Fish were plentiful and there were good markets. In a cosmopolitan area, with soldiers, wayfarers, pilgrims and pedlars coming and going, as well as the local population, people would always want what they were selling. But it was hard work, and sometimes dangerous. Their lives were hardly luxurious, but were modestly secure.

So why did they give it all up to follow a wandering preacher?

The same question faces people today. Why did this person give up a promising legal career to become a preacher, throwing away a lifetime of high earnings for the insecurity and poverty of pastoring and teaching a church? Why did that person abandon her remarkable gift as a singer in order to study theology and get ordained? Why did this person become a teacher, that one a prison governor, this one a monk, that one a missionary? And – since these more obvious callings are only the tip of the iceberg of Christian vocation – why do Christians in millions of other walks of life regularly give up lifestyles and practices that look attractive and lucrative in order to maintain honesty, integrity, faith, hope and love?

The answer can only be in Jesus himself, and in the astonishing magnetism of his presence and personality. This can be known and felt today, as we meditate on the stories about him and pray to know him better, just as the first disciples knew and felt his presence 2,000 years ago. Sometimes his call comes slowly, starting like a faint murmur and growing until we can no longer ignore it. Sometimes he calls people as suddenly and dramatically as he called Peter and Andrew, James and John. When that happens to you, by whatever means and at whatever pace, you will know; Jesus has a way of getting through, and whatever we are engaged with – whatever nets we are mending, or fish we are catching – somehow we will be sufficiently aware of his presence and call to know what it is we're being asked to do.

At least, we will know we're being asked to follow him. We won't necessarily know where it's all going to lead, and we wouldn't perhaps be quite so eager if we did. 'You'll be catching people now!' was what Jesus said to Peter and Andrew; what did they think that would mean? Did they know how the 'people' in question would feel about it? Did they have any inkling that both of them would end up being crucified, as their master would be? Did James, the brother of John, have the slightest idea that within a few years he would be dead, killed on the orders of Herod?

No, they didn't. God in his mercy reveals things little by little. Nor did Peter think that he would end up with a huge church in Rome dedicated to his memory; or Andrew suppose that whole countries (Scotland, Greece, Russia) would regard him as their patron saint. They saw neither the glory nor the pain that day when a young man walked by the sea in their little town of Capernaum, on the north shore of the Sea of Galilee. They only saw him; and that was enough. In him, as Paul might have said, all the treasures of glory and pain are hidden. That is what the gospel story is all about.

But it wasn't just personal magnetism that drew people from hundreds of miles around to seek out this Jesus as he went to and fro across the region of Galilee. It was his remarkable healings. Matthew will tell us more stories about such events in due course. For the moment, in quick summary fashion, he tells us how word suddenly went out that people whose lives had been blighted by every kind of illness and disease – and we only have to think for a minute of life before modern medicine to realize what that would mean – could be healed if they came to this extraordinary man.

Historians today are agreed that this is the only explanation for the crowds Jesus drew. He really did have remarkable powers of healing. But Jesus was never simply a healer pure and simple, vital though that was as part of his work. For him, the healings were signs of the new thing that God was doing through him. God's kingdom – God's sovereign, saving rule – was at last being unleashed upon Israel and the world, through him. How could this not bring healing in its wake? Soon the fishermen found themselves, not placidly working at their family craft beside the lake, but at the centre of bustling crowds. Jesus' mission was well and truly launched, and they were caught up in it.

What pulls in the crowds today? Entertainment, of course: football, rock music, big fireworks parties. And great national tragedies, such as the death of a popular princess, or a major disaster. What would it take – what could and should Jesus' followers be doing today – that would send people off with the word that something new was happening and that everyone should come quickly?

For reflection or discussion

- In what ways do Jesus' presence and personality continue to attract and call people to follow him today?
- The passage suggests that Jesus' healings were not only acts of compassion and restoration but also signs of the new thing that God was doing through him, ushering in God's kingdom. How can today's followers of Jesus engage in acts that signify the arrival of something new and transformative, compelling others to take notice and be drawn towards faith?

Tuesday

The healing of a paralysed man: Mark 2.1–12

[1]Jesus went back again to Capernaum, where, after a few days, word got round that he was at home. [2]A crowd gathered, so that

people couldn't even get near the door as he was telling them the message.

³A party arrived: four people carrying a paralysed man, bringing him to Jesus. ⁴They couldn't get through to him because of the crowd, so they opened up the roof above where he was. When they had dug through it, they used ropes to let down the stretcher on which the paralysed man was lying.

⁵Jesus saw their faith, and said to the paralysed man, 'Child, your sins are forgiven!'

⁶'How dare the fellow speak like this?' grumbled some of the legal experts among themselves. ⁷'It's blasphemy! Who can forgive sins except God?'

⁸Jesus knew at once, in his spirit, that thoughts like this were in the air. 'Why do your hearts tell you to think that?' he asked. ⁹'Answer me this,' he went on. 'Is it easier to say to this cripple, "Your sins are forgiven", or to say, "Get up, pick up your stretcher, and walk"?

¹⁰'You want to know that the son of man has authority on earth to forgive sins?' He turned to the paralytic. ¹¹'I tell you,' he said, 'Get up, take your stretcher, and go home.' ¹²He got up, picked up the stretcher in a flash, and went out before them all. Everyone was astonished, and they praised God. 'We've never seen anything like this!' they said.

Most people don't realize that this was probably Jesus' own house. He had moved to Capernaum from Nazareth; the point of the first two verses is that when Jesus returned from his short preaching trip around the neighbouring villages, he found crowds pressing around the door as though he were a movie star or well-known footballer. Jesus himself was the unlucky householder who had his roof ruined that day.

This opens up quite a new possibility for understanding what Jesus said to the paralysed man. How would you feel if someone made a big hole in your roof? But Jesus looks down and says, with a rueful smile: 'All right – I forgive you!' Something in his voice, though, made them all realize this was different. This forgiveness went deeper than mere domestic disputes. Jesus was speaking with a quiet authority which went down into the paralysed man's innermost being. Not surprisingly, those around felt uneasy. Only the priests could declare forgiveness, speaking in the name of God. If that's what the man needed, his friends should take him to the Temple in Jerusalem, not to a wandering preacher.

Mark's way of telling the tale makes it a signpost. It points on, through the twists and turns of the gospel story, to Jesus' trial before Caiaphas in chapter 14. The story is a tiny version of the whole gospel: Jesus teaching and healing, Jesus condemned for blasphemy, Jesus vindicated. The paralysed man's healing points forward to the new life that Jesus himself will have in the resurrection, and will share with everyone who wants it.

The key sentence, then, is the one in verse 10: 'The son of man has authority on earth to forgive sins.' 'The son of man', in Jesus' language, could simply mean 'I', or 'someone like me'. But taking 'the son of man' in Mark as a whole, Daniel 7 provides the clue to deeper meaning. There, 'one like a son of man' is the representative of God's true people. He is opposed by the forces of evil; but God vindicates him, rescues him, proves him to be in the right, and gives him *authority*. In Daniel, this authority enables him to dispense God's judgment. Here, in a fascinating twist, he has authority to dispense God's forgiveness. The saying points forward to Jesus' answer to Caiaphas (14.62).

In many cultures today, forgiveness is seen as a sign of weakness. Revenge, for them, is a moral duty. Sometimes whole families, whole communities, are torn apart this way. 'It's the only language they understand,' people say, as they plant another bomb or aim another rifle. Sometimes whole nations and governments engage in childish, but deadly, tit-for-tat retaliations. People who live that way tend to think that God lives that way too.

We shouldn't be surprised, then, that Jesus' unexpected declaration of forgiveness sent shock waves running through the house, the village, the nation, and finally through the world. It wasn't simply that he was committing a theological crime. The hole in his own roof was nothing compared with the hole he was tearing through an entire way of life. Forgiveness is the most powerful thing in the world, but because it is so costly we prefer to settle for second best. Jesus, already on his way to paying the full price, offered nothing less than the best.

Jesus' people have to be for the world what he was for Israel. We have to find ways of bringing healing and forgiveness to our communities. It can be done – think of the Truth and Reconciliation Commission in South Africa – but it is enormously costly. People will oppose it. But the new life that comes as a result is enough vindication, enough proof that the living God is at work.

Forgiveness can also, of course, change individuals. It can, as in this case, go down to the hidden roots of the personality, gently healing old, long-buried, hurts. Often people think healing and forgiveness is impossible. They find God distant or uncaring. But true faith won't be satisfied with that. This story is a picture of prayer. Don't stay on the edge of the crowd. Dig through God's roof and find yourself in his presence.

You will get more than you bargained for. Once you've met the living, forgiving God in Jesus, you'll find yourself on your feet, going out into the world in the power of God's love.

For reflection or discussion

- In what ways does forgiveness demonstrate strength rather than weakness?
- What does it mean for Jesus' followers to embody his example of bringing healing and forgiveness into the world, and what are the challenges associated with this task today?

Wednesday

Jairus's daughter and a woman with chronic bleeding: Luke 8.40–56

[40]A large crowd was waiting for Jesus. [41]A man named Jairus, a ruler of the synagogue, came and fell down in front of his feet. He pleaded with him to come to his house, [42]because he had an only daughter, twelve years old, who was dying. So they set off, and the crowd pressed close in around him.

[43]There was a woman who had had an internal haemorrhage for twelve years. She had spent all she had on doctors, but had not been able to find a cure from anyone. [44]She came up behind Jesus and touched the hem of his robe. Immediately her flow of blood dried up.

[45]'Who touched me?' asked Jesus.

Everybody denied it. 'Master,' said Peter, 'the crowds are crushing you and pressing you!'

[46]'Somebody touched me,' said Jesus. 'Power went out from me, and I knew it.'

[47]When the woman saw that she couldn't remain hidden, she came up, trembling, and fell down in front of him. She told him, in front of everyone, why she had touched him, and how she had been healed instantly.

[48]'Daughter,' said Jesus, 'your faith has saved you. Go in peace.'

[49]While he was still speaking, someone arrived from the synagogue-ruler's house. 'Your daughter's dead,' he said. 'Don't bother the teacher any longer.'

[50]'Don't be afraid,' said Jesus when he heard it. 'Just believe, and she will be rescued.'

[51]When they got to the house, he didn't let anyone come in with them except Peter, John and James, and the child's father and mother. [52]Everyone was weeping and wailing for her.

'Don't cry,' said Jesus. 'She isn't dead; she's asleep.' [53]They laughed at him, knowing that she was dead.

[54]But he took her by the hand. 'Get up, child,' he called. [55]Her spirit returned, and she got up at once. He told them to give her something to eat. [56]Her parents were astounded, but he told them to tell nobody what had happened.

We don't know for sure that Luke was a doctor, though there are several things in his work that make it likely, as well as Paul's mention of him as 'Luke, the beloved doctor' (Colossians 4.14). But if he was, there must have been a wry smile on his face when he wrote verse 43. Perhaps he knew of patients like that, who had spent everything they had on medical attention and it still didn't make any difference. In a world without modern medicine, and also without any form of state-funded medical aid or private insurance schemes, good health was a precious but fragile commodity. If you didn't have it, you might easily find that sickness and poverty followed each other in a downward spiral from which no return was possible.

Luke has followed Mark in fitting the story of the woman and her twelve-year ailment inside the story of Jairus's twelve-year-old daughter. The two parts of the story are joined in several other ways, too, particularly in Jesus' command to Jairus to have faith, which comes immediately after he has told the woman that her faith has brought her salvation. If Jairus's faith was to help in the healing of his daughter, then that faith was itself helped by seeing Jesus declare that power had gone out from him even before he knew who had been healed. (The phrase itself is striking, and says a lot about what it was like for Jesus to be instrumental in so much healing.) If touching Jesus could have that effect, who knew what might happen if Jesus himself came and touched a dead little girl?

Of course, touching was itself very important in both cases. In the world before modern hygiene (soap as we know it wasn't invented until the Middle Ages, and of course many things we take for granted today, such as running water and proper drains, were barely thought of then), purity taboos were vital simply to maintain public health. The Jewish scriptures and subsequent traditions had codified and elaborated them into almost an art form. And two of the most obvious sources of pollution were corpses, and women with internal bleeding.

In other words, a first-century reader coming upon this double story would know very well that Jesus was, apparently, incurring double pollution. In the first case he couldn't help it; the woman came and touched him without his knowing either that she was doing it or what she was suffering from; but officially he had become 'unclean' none the less. That is partly why the woman hoped to remain hidden, and why she was shy about coming forward, and then crushingly embarrassed when eventually she had to. In the second case, though, Jesus deliberately went and touched a dead body.

In both cases, the woman and the girl, we find further signs of Luke's care about, and interest in, the stories of women; as is well known, he highlights their role more than the other gospels. But in both, as well, we also find foreshadowings of what is to come in Jesus' story. Luke has been patiently pointing out, through one story after another, who Jesus really is. He is also, at the same time, opening the way for his central explanation of what Jesus has come to achieve. When Luke tells of Jesus' arrival in Jerusalem, and his arrest and death, his main theme is of how Jesus, innocent of anything that would condemn him to crucifixion, takes the place of the guilty, those who had courted that fate all along. Already in these incidents we see the same pattern emerging. Jesus shares the pollution of sickness and death, but the power of his own love – and it is love, above all, that shines through these stories – turns that pollution into wholeness and hope.

This is the message that Luke would repeat to us today, in whatever problem or suffering we face. The presence of Jesus, getting his hands dirty with the problems of the world, is what we need, and what in the gospel we are promised. As we live inside Luke's developing story, we find Jesus quietly coming alongside us in our own muddle and fear. He welcomes our trembling touch, and responds with that central biblical command: 'Don't be afraid.'

For reflection or discussion

- In what ways does Luke's portrayal of Jesus being touched by the woman and touching the dead girl challenge social and religious norms of purity and pollution in the first century?
- Reflecting on Luke's interest in stories of women, and in Jesus' willingness to engage with those considered unclean or marginalized, what does this tell you about Jesus' mission?

Thursday

The feeding of the five thousand: Matthew 14.10, 12–21

[10]Herod sent to the prison and had John beheaded . . . [12]His disciples came and took away the body and buried it. Then they went and told Jesus.

[13]When Jesus heard it, he went away from there in a boat to a deserted spot by himself. The crowds heard about it, and they followed him on foot from the towns. [14]When he came out and saw the large crowd, he was sorry for them. He healed their sick.

[15]When it was evening, the disciples came to him.

'This is a deserted spot,' they said, 'and it's already getting late. Send the crowds away so that they can go into the villages and buy food for themselves.'

[16]'They don't need to go away,' said Jesus. 'You give them something to eat.'

[17]'All we have here', they said, 'is five loaves of bread and two fish.'

[18]'Bring them here to me,' he said.

[19]He told the crowds to sit down on the grass. Then he took the five loaves and the two fish and looked up to heaven. He blessed the loaves, broke them, and gave them to the disciples, and the disciples gave them to the crowds. [20]Everybody ate and was satisfied, and they picked up twelve baskets full of broken pieces. [21]There were about five thousand men who had eaten, besides women and children.

Come and be a character in this story. There's plenty of room, and there's a lot to learn.

To begin with, cast your mind back to the last time you were really, really sad. After the death of a parent, perhaps, or a close friend. After you didn't get the job you'd set your heart on. After you had to move out of the house you had loved. What you needed and wanted most was to hide away and be quiet. To reflect, perhaps to pray; but above all to be still, and not have people bother you.

Then supposing the quiet place you chose was invaded by hundreds of others. The little church you thought you'd slip inside was full of a wedding party. The lonely hillside where, surely, you could be private was covered in cheerful hikers. How would you react?

Jesus' reaction here is the more remarkable. He had lost John, his cousin and colleague. He had lost him in a manner which must have warned Jesus of what lay ahead for him, too. Yet when he slips away to be quiet and alone, the crowds discover and throng all around him. And his reaction is not anger or frustration, but compassion. He translates his sorrow over John, and perhaps his sorrow over himself, into sorrow for them. Before the outward and visible works of power, healing the sick, comes the inward and invisible work of power, in which Jesus transforms his own feelings into love for those in need.

You have come into the story of Jesus, perhaps, because you've been touched yourself by that compassion. Imagine yourself as one of the disciples – not a leader, just one of the Twelve, or perhaps one of their other friends or cousins, hanging around on the edge. You see how Jesus cares for people, and you'd like to care for them too. So you think what might be best for them, and come to him with a suggestion. Wouldn't it be good to send them away now, so that they can go and buy food rather than all getting hungry here, miles away from anywhere? Jesus is always delighted when people around him come up with ideas which show that they're thinking of the needs of others. But often what he has to do is to take those ideas and do something startling with them. If you really care for them, he says, why don't *you* give them something to eat? This is, perhaps, the typical note of vocation. Our small idea of how to care for people gets bounced back at us with what seems a huge and impossible proposal. You protest. I can't do it! I haven't got the time. I haven't got the energy. I haven't got the ability. All I have is . . .

Ah, but that's the next step, and again typical of how God's calling works. By hanging around Jesus, you've had an idea. It isn't quite in focus, but your main intention – in this case, that the people should be fed – is on target. Jesus proposes achieving that aim by a different means. You say it's impossible – *but you're prepared to give him the little you've got, if it'll be any good.* Of course it means you'll go hungry yourself . . . but by now you're in too deep to stop. Once the power of Jesus' compassion has begun to catch you up in its flow, you can't stop.

What precisely Jesus does with what we give him is so mysterious and powerful that it's hard to describe in words. Imagine yourself standing there, while Jesus, surrounded by thousands of people, takes this pitifully small amount of food, hardly enough for two people, let alone a crowd, and prays over it. He thanks God for it. He breaks it, and gives it to you and the others, and you give it to . . . one person after another after another, without knowing what's happening or how.

Think through how it's happened. Being close to Jesus has turned into the thought of service; Jesus takes the thought, turns it inside out (making it more costly, of course), and gives it back to you as a challenge. In puzzled response to the challenge, you offer what you've got, knowing it's quite inadequate (but again costly); and the same thing happens. He takes it, blesses it, and breaks it (there's the cost, yet again), and gives it to you – and your job now is to give it to everybody else.

This is how it works whenever someone is close enough to Jesus to catch a glimpse of what he's doing and how they could help. We blunder in with our ideas. We offer, uncomprehending, what little we have. Jesus takes ideas, loaves and fishes, money, a sense of humour, time, energy, talents, love, artistic gifts, skill with words, quickness of eye or fingers, whatever we have to offer. He holds them before his father with prayer and blessing. Then, breaking them so they are ready for use, he gives them back to us to give to those who need them.

And now they are both ours and not ours. They are both what we had in mind and not what we had in mind. Something greater and different, more powerful and mysterious, yet also our own. It is part of genuine Christian service, at whatever level, that we look on in amazement to see what God has done with the bits and pieces we dug out of our meagre resources to offer to him.

Within Matthew's story, of course, there is much more going on than simply a remarkable example of Christian vocation. The twelve baskets left over may point to Jesus' intention to restore God's people, the twelve tribes of Israel. Jesus feeding people in the wilderness fits so well with Matthew's theme of Jesus as the new Moses (God gave the Israelites manna, special bread from heaven, when they were in the desert in the time of Moses) that we can be sure Matthew intended us to see this too.

This probably explains why Jesus sent the crowds away as soon as the feeding was over. He didn't want them hanging around and celebrating his power. The likeness with Moses stops there. Jesus was not intending to march through the land at the head of a great crowd, or to win military victories against God's enemies. He was going to achieve at last the loneliness he sought at the start of this passage, hanging desolate on a cross. If you sense a call to follow him, to share his compassion, to give him what you have so that it can be used in his service, you must remember that it cost him everything as well.

For reflection or discussion

- Reflect on a time when you felt the need to be alone and find solace in a quiet place. How would you have reacted if that solitude was interrupted by a large gathering of people seeking your attention? How does Jesus' compassionate response in a similar situation inform your own understanding of service and selflessness?

- How does this passage illustrate the process of becoming close to Jesus, receiving a challenge, offering what we have, and witnessing to the mysterious and powerful work of God in transforming and multiplying our contributions?

Friday

Bread from heaven: John 6.14–35

[14]When the people saw the sign that Jesus had done, they said, 'This really is the Prophet, the one who is to come into the world.' [15]So when Jesus realized that they were intending to come and seize him to make him king, he withdrew again, by himself, up the mountain.

[16]When it was evening, Jesus' disciples went down to the seashore. [17]They got into a boat, and went across the sea towards Capernaum. It was already getting dark, and Jesus had not yet come to them. [18]A strong wind blew up, and the sea began to get rough. [19]They had been rowing for about three or four miles when they saw Jesus walking on the sea, coming towards the boat. They were terrified.

²⁰But he spoke to them.

'It's me!' he said. 'Don't be afraid!'

²¹Then they were eager to take him into the boat; and at once the boat arrived at the land they had been making for.

²²The next day the crowd that had remained on the far side of the lake saw that there had only been the one boat there. They knew that Jesus hadn't gone with his disciples, but that the disciples had set off by themselves. ²³But other boats came from Tiberias, near the place where they had eaten the bread after the Lord had given thanks. ²⁴When the crowd saw that neither Jesus nor his disciples were there, they themselves got into the boats and came to Capernaum looking for Jesus.

²⁵When they found him beside the sea, they said to him, 'Rabbi, when did you get here?'

²⁶This was Jesus' reply:

'I'm telling you the solemn truth,' he said. 'You aren't looking for me because you saw signs, but because you ate as much bread as you could. ²⁷You shouldn't be working for perishable food, but for food that will last to the life of God's coming age – the food which the son of man will give you, the person whom God the father has stamped with the seal of his approval.'

²⁸'What should we be doing,' they asked him, 'so that we can be doing the work God wants?'

²⁹'This is the work God wants of you,' replied Jesus, 'that you believe in the one he sent.'

³⁰'Well, then,' they said to him, 'what sign are you going to do, so that we can see it and believe you? What work are you doing? ³¹Our ancestors ate the manna in the wilderness; it says in the Bible that "he gave them bread from heaven to eat".'

³²'I'm telling you the solemn truth,' Jesus replied. 'It wasn't Moses who gave you the bread from heaven. It was my father who gave you the true bread from heaven. ³³God's bread, you see, is the one who comes down from heaven and gives life to the world.'

[34]'Master,' they said, 'give us this bread – give it to us always!'

[35]'I am the bread of life,' replied Jesus. 'Anyone who comes to me will never be hungry!'

The historian was in a hurry to finish his PhD. There was one chapter to go, which concerned the paintings that had been so important during his period, and the influence the artists had had on the wider thought and culture of the time.

He went hastily from gallery to gallery. In every room he walked around beside the walls, scribbling in his notebook, taking down all the details from the printed notices underneath the paintings. He wrote down the artists' names, their dates, where they lived, the names of their key paintings, who their friends were, what influence others had had on them, and they on others. As soon as he was finished he went on to the next gallery.

He finished his PhD. But at no time, in all the art galleries, had he ever stood back and looked at the paintings themselves, and allowed them to speak in their own language.

Jesus is clearly anxious that the people whom he fed with the loaves and fishes are going to end up like that unfortunate historian. The printed notes were there to lead the eye, the mind and the heart to appreciate the paintings, not so that they could be used in a purely mechanical fashion of processing information. The bread and the fish that Jesus had distributed to the crowds were there to lead the eye, the mind and the heart to the true gift of God to his people, then and there. They were there to open up their understanding to the fact that the new Passover, the new Exodus, was taking place right in front of them, and that Jesus was leading it.

At first sight Jesus' warning seems almost churlish. He has done something remarkable; they are excited and come to him wanting more; and he all but rebukes them for having the wrong motivation. What else could you expect from them? But underneath the warning of verses 26 and 27 is his recognition that after the feeding in the wilderness they were only a moment away from making him king (verse 15) – and they would have meant him to be a king like other kings, a strong this-worldly figure who would lead them in their strong this-worldly agendas. Jesus is indeed a king, but the type and manner of his kingship will be very different from what the crowds expected or wanted.

Here his charge against the crowds is that the 'sign' of the feeding is meant to lead you to the true food: the food the son of man will give (verse 27), the food which *is* Jesus himself (verse 35). What matters is not just what Jesus can do for you; what matters is who Jesus *is*. Only if you're prepared to be confronted by that in a new way can you begin to understand what he can really do for you, what he really wants to do for you. Only if the eager note-taker is prepared to stop and ask what these signs are *for* can he ever pause, lift his eyes and enter into the actual world of the artist instead of remaining in the world of the hurried would-be scholar.

The question of who Jesus really is now comes to the fore. First, he is the one upon whom the father has set his seal (verse 27): God, like a goldsmith with a hallmark, or like a king with his great seal, has stamped this person with the mark that declares not only where he comes from but that he carries his authority. What Jesus is doing, in other words, bears the marks that say: this is the kind of thing that, in Israel's scriptures, God himself does. The wilderness feeding and the walking on water speak of this in ways that, though quite different, are both related to the Exodus story.

Second, God is making a demand on them – the crowd realize that Jesus is pointing out that they can't just expect bread on demand, that if this really is a heaven-sent renewal movement there will be a new standard to which they must sign up. This means that God is making a demand on them, and it is this: that they believe in Jesus. No new exposition of the detailed commandments of the law; rather, a command which, if it is to be obeyed, will require a change of heart.

It will require, in particular, the recognition that in Jesus, and in everything he is doing, the same God is at work who was at work in the Exodus story. It seems odd that they ask for a further sign, when Jesus has just given them one. Perhaps they were hoping for something more obviously military and political. Perhaps they wanted Jesus to march on Jerusalem and make the walls fall down, as Joshua had done with Jericho at the conclusion of the Exodus. Jesus doesn't answer their request for a further sign, but instead points out that the real answer to their question is standing in front of them. Moses was only God's agent. What was going on, all along, was that God was providing not just the physical bread dropping down from the sky (Exodus 16), but the spiritual nourishment which kept alive their faith and hope. That was what God was doing then, and that was what he was doing now.

The passage ends, climactically, with the first of the famous 'I am' sayings in John's gospel (verse 35). It is another way of saying what the Prologue said: Jesus is the Word, the one who comes from the father into the world to accomplish his purpose. And in this case the particular emphasis is on nourishment. Until they recognize who Jesus really is, they may be fed with bread and fish, but there is a deep hunger inside them which will never be satisfied. Verse 34 can be used to this day, as it stands, as the prayer that we all need to pray if our deepest needs are to be met.

For reflection or discussion

- Consider the warning Jesus gives to the crowds about their motivations and expectations regarding his kingship. Do you ever try to mould Jesus into your own image rather than submitting to his true identity and purpose?
- How does the image of Jesus as the bread of life speak to your deepest needs and longings? How can you cultivate a genuine recognition of who Jesus is and allow him to satisfy the hunger within you?

Saturday

Jesus heals a blind beggar: Mark 10.46–52

[46]They came to Jericho. As Jesus, his disciples and a substantial crowd were leaving the town, a blind beggar named Bartimaeus, the son of Timaeus, was sitting by the road. [47]When he heard it was Jesus of Nazareth, he began to shout out: 'Son of David! Jesus! Take pity on me!'

[48]Lots of people told him crossly to be quiet. But he shouted out all the louder, 'Son of David – take pity on me!'

[49]Jesus came to a stop. 'Call him,' he said.

So they called the blind man.

'Cheer up,' they said, 'and get up. He's calling you.'

[50]He flung his cloak aside, jumped up, and came to Jesus.

Jesus saw him coming. [51]'What do you want me to do for you?' he asked.

'Teacher,' the blind man said, 'let me see again.'

[52]'Off you go,' said Jesus. 'Your faith has saved you.' And immediately he saw again, and he followed him on the way.

It took some weeks of persuasion before they came to see me. The grown-up son was desperate to get his ailing and depressed mother into some kind of a home where she would be properly cared for. As long as she lived with him he couldn't do his own work or have any private life. She swamped him with demands for help and attention. We looked at several options. There were small communities, large communities, nursing homes, sheltered housing. Any of them would have been real possibilities. The mother, though, saw some flaw in each of them which became, to her, fatal. None of them would do. After an hour she turned to the son with triumph gleaming in her eyes. 'There you are!' she said. 'He can't do anything for us.'

But the truth was that she didn't *want* anybody to do anything for her. She wanted to go on being a victim, putting moral pressure on her son (and everybody else in sight) to feel sorry for her.

Jesus' question to Bartimaeus addresses exactly that possibility. 'What do you want me to do for you?' Do you, Bartimaeus, want to give up begging? Do you want to have to live differently, to work for a living, to have no reason to sit by the roadside all day whining at passers-by? It's quite a challenge, and Bartimaeus rises to it splendidly. He wants the new life; not only sight, but the chance to follow Jesus. Fancy seeing for the first time for many years, and imagine that the first thing you saw was Jesus on his way up to Jerusalem.

Mark is quite clear: Bartimaeus is a model to imitate. Unlike the disciples, who hadn't really understood what Jesus was about, he is already a man of faith, courage and true discipleship. He recognizes who Jesus is ('son of David'); he clearly believes Jesus can help him ('your faith has saved you'); he leaves his begging (the cloak would be spread on the ground to receive money; Jericho is seldom cold enough for anyone to wear a cloak during the day), and he follows Jesus on the way ('the way' was the early Christians' term for what we call 'Christianity').

He makes a stark contrast with the disciples. Remember how, when Jesus said to James and John, 'What do you want me to do for you?', all he got was a request for power, prestige and glory. As with the blind man in chapter 8, the healing of Bartimaeus is a sign that Jesus is trying to open his followers' eyes, this time to see him not just as Messiah but as the one who would give his life to bring salvation to all.

When Jesus says 'Your faith has saved you', the word 'saved' refers to physical healing (compare 5.34). For any early Christian, though, it would have carried a wider and deeper meaning as well. The different dimensions of salvation were not sharply distinguished either by Jesus or by the gospel writers. God's rescue of people from what we think of as physical ailments on the one hand and spiritual peril on the other were thought of as different aspects of the same event. But we see that the key to salvation, of whatever kind, is faith. That's why anyone, even those normally excluded from pure or polite society, can be saved. Faith is open to all; and often it's the unexpected people who seem to have it most strongly. And faith consists not least in recognizing who Jesus is and trusting that he has the power to rescue.

This is the kind of story that lends itself particularly well to slow, patient meditation. Take some time and imagine yourself in the crowd that day in Jericho. It's hot, dry and dusty (it almost always is there). You're excited; you're with Jesus; you're going up to Jerusalem. And here is someone shouting from the roadside. It's a nuisance. It's possibly even dangerous (if enough people call him 'son of David', someone in authority is going to get alarmed). Examine your own feelings. Try to remember other times when you've felt like that. Then watch as Jesus, never put out by what annoys his followers, turns to speak to the blind man. How do you feel about that? Do you want this beggar in the party? How about when Jesus speaks warm and welcoming words to him? Has he ever spoken to you like that? How do you feel as you set off together up the hill to Jerusalem?

Now imagine yourself as the blind man. We all have something, by no means necessarily a physical ailment, that we know is getting in the way of our being the people we believe God wants us to be and made us to be. Sit by the roadside and listen to the crowd. Examine your own feelings when you discover it's Jesus coming by. Call out to him, and when he summons you, put everything aside and go to him. And when he asks you what you want him to do, go for it. Don't look back at the small, selfish comforts of victimhood. Ask for freedom, for salvation. And when you get it, be prepared to follow Jesus wherever he goes next.

For reflection or discussion

- Imagine yourself in this story as either a member of the crowd or as the blind man. How does it feel to witness Jesus' interaction with Bartimaeus? How does it challenge your own prejudices, preconceptions and desires?

• Reflect on the areas of limitation or hindrance that prevent you from fully embracing the person God created you to be. How can you call out to Jesus, ask for freedom and salvation, and be ready to follow him wherever he leads?

Week 2
Jesus in prayer

Monday

The Lord's Prayer: Matthew 5.1–2; 6.5–15

[1]When Jesus saw the crowds, he went up the hillside, and sat down. His disciples came to him. [2]He took a deep breath, and began his teaching . . .

[5]'When you pray, you mustn't be like the play-actors. They love to pray standing in the synagogues and on street corners, so that people will notice them. I'm telling you the truth: they have received their reward in full. [6]No: when you pray, go into your own room, shut the door, and pray to your father who is there in secret. And your father, who sees in secret, will repay you.

[7]'When you pray, don't pile up a jumbled heap of words! That's what the Gentiles do. They reckon that the more they say, the more likely they are to be heard. [8]So don't be like them. You see, your father knows what you need before you ask him.

[9]'So this is how you should pray:
Our father in heaven,
may your name be honoured.
[10]May your kingdom come.
May your will be done,
as in heaven, so on earth.
[11]Give us today the bread we need now;
[12]and forgive us the things we owe,
as we too have forgiven what was owed to us.

[13]Don't bring us into the great trial,
but rescue us from evil.
[14]'Yes: if you forgive people the wrong they have done, your heavenly father will forgive you as well. [15]But if you don't forgive people, neither will your heavenly father forgive you what you have done wrong.'

I was talking to a friend who had the reputation of being one of the finest preachers in the area. How did he go about it, I asked? He had no particular technique, he said; he just puzzled over the biblical readings that were set for that day until a framework emerged. Once he'd got a framework it was just a matter of writing it out.

That, of course, was a deceptively simple answer, and we can only guess at the hours of struggle and prayer that were disguised by such a short, and humble, response. But it's often the case, in many areas of life, that we blunder around until we find a framework on which we can build. And this is almost always true with prayer.

Jesus contrasts the sort of praying he has in mind with the sort that went on in much of the non-Jewish world. We know from many writings and inscriptions that many non-Jews did indeed use multiple formulae in their prayers: long, complicated magic words which they would repeat over and over in their anxiety to persuade some god or goddess to be favourable to them. Such prayers are often marked by a note of uncertainty. There were many divinities in the ancient pagan world, and nobody quite knew which one might need pacifying next, or with what formula.

This is hardly surprising. Prayer is one of life's great mysteries. Most people pray at least sometimes; some people, in many very different religious traditions, pray a great deal. At its lowest, prayer is shouting into a void on the off-chance there may be someone out there listening. At its highest, prayer merges into love, as the presence of God becomes so real that we pass beyond words and into a sense of his reality, generosity, delight and grace. For most Christians, most of the time, it takes place somewhere in between those two extremes. To be frank, for many people it is not just a mystery but a puzzle. They know they ought to do it but they aren't quite sure how.

What the Lord's Prayer provides, here at the heart of the Sermon on the Mount, is a *framework*. Jesus doesn't say you should always use identical words, and actually when Luke gives his version of the prayer it is different in small but interesting ways (Luke 11.2–4). It looks as though Jesus intended this sequence of thought to act more like the scaffolding than the whole building, though of course the prayer is used as it stands by countless Christians every day. Already by Jesus' day the Jewish patterns of prayer were well established, with short but powerful prayers to be said three times a day. Maybe Jesus intended this prayer to be used like that as well.

What then does the prayer tell us about our regular approach to God? First, and so obvious that we might miss it, the prayer is deeply *meaningful*. It isn't a magic formula, an 'abracadabra', which plugs into some secret charm or spell. It is something we can mean with our minds (though it will stretch our thinking) as well as say with our lips. It implies strongly that we humans can and should use our ordinary language in talking to the creator of the universe, and that he wants and intends us to do so. It implies, in other words, that we share with the one true God a world of meaning which he wants us to explore.

Second, everything is set within our calling God 'father'. For Jews in Jesus' day, this title for God went back to God's action in the Exodus, rescuing Israel from Egypt and so demonstrating that 'Israel is my son, my firstborn' (Exodus 4.22).

Third, this God is not a man-made idol. He is the living God, who dwells in 'heaven', and longs to see his sovereign and saving rule come to birth on 'earth'. This is, in fact, a prayer for the kingdom of God to become fully present: not for God's people to be snatched away from earth to heaven, but for the glory and beauty of heaven to be turned into earthly reality as well. When that is done,

God's name – his character, his reputation, his very presence – will be held in high honour everywhere. The first half of the prayer is thus all about God. Prayer that doesn't start there is always in danger of concentrating on ourselves, and very soon it stops being prayer altogether and collapses into the random thoughts, fears and longings of our own minds.

Fourth, though, because this God is the creator, who loves his world and his human creatures, we can ask him for everything we need in the safe knowledge that he is far more concerned about it all even than we are ourselves. Much of the rest of the chapter spells this out. But if we are truly praying this prayer to God's honour, we can never simply pray for food for ourselves. We must pray for the needs of the whole world, where millions go hungry and many starve. And already we may sense, bubbling up out of the prayer, the realization that if we truly pray it we might also have to do something about it, to become part of God's answer to our own praying.

Fifth, we pray for forgiveness. Unlike some religions, in which every single action carries eternal and unbreakable consequences, at the heart of Judaism and Christianity lies the belief that, though human actions matter very deeply, forgiveness is possible and, through God's love, can become actual. Jesus assumes that we will need to ask for forgiveness not on one or two rare occasions but very regularly. This is a sobering thought, but it is matched by the comforting news that forgiveness is freely available as often as we need it.

There is, however, a condition, which remarkably enough is brought right into the prayer itself: we ourselves must be forgiving people. Jesus takes an extra moment afterwards to explain why. The heart that will not open to forgive others will remain closed when God's own forgiveness is offered.

The prayer ends with a sombre and realistic note. Jesus believed that the great time of testing was coming upon the world, and that he would have to walk alone into its darkness. His followers should pray to be spared it. Even now, in the light of Easter and with the guidance and power of the holy spirit, we still need to pray in this way. There will come yet more times of crisis, times when all seems dark for the world, the church, and in our own hearts and lives. If we follow a crucified Messiah, we shouldn't expect to be spared the darkness ourselves. But we must, and may, pray to be kept from its worst ravages, and to be delivered from evil, both in the abstract and in its personified form, 'the evil one'.

Here is the framework Jesus knew we would need. Here is your heavenly father waiting and longing for you to use it day by day as you grow in your knowledge, love and service of him. What is stopping you from making it your own?

For reflection or discussion

- How does the Lord's Prayer provide a framework for approaching God? What aspects of the prayer emphasize your relationship with God and your responsibility to others?
- The prayer emphasizes the importance of forgiveness, both in seeking forgiveness from God and extending it to others. Why do you think forgiveness is highlighted in this prayer? How does it relate to your spiritual well-being and your ability to experience God's forgiveness?

Tuesday

In the presence of God: Matthew 11.25–30

[25]At that time Jesus turned to God with this prayer: 'I give you my praise, father, Lord of heaven and earth! You hid these things from the wise and intelligent and revealed them to children! [26]Yes, father, that's the way you decided to do it! [27]My father gave me everything: nobody knows the son except the father, and nobody knows the father except the son – and anyone the son wants to reveal him to.

[28]'Are you having a real struggle? Come to me! Are you carrying a big load on your back? Come to me – I'll give you a rest! [29]Pick up my yoke and put it on; take lessons from me! My heart is gentle, not arrogant. You'll find the rest you deeply need. [30]My yoke is easy to wear, my load is easy to bear.'

I was present at the memorial service to honour one of the world's great sportsmen. Colin Cowdrey was one of the greatest cricketers of all time; not quite cricket's Babe Ruth, but not far off. He was known and loved all around the world – not least in India, Australia, Pakistan and the West Indies, whose cricketers had learned to fear and respect his extraordinary ability, and whose crowds had come to love him as a man, not just as a player.

The service was magnificent. Tributes flowed in from around the world; a former prime minister gave the main address; a special song had been written. But for me the most moving moment was when one of Cowdrey's sons came forward and spoke of his father from his inside knowledge. This great public figure, who gave of himself in later life to every good cause he could find, had never lost his close and intimate love for his children and grandchildren. There were many fine stories which only a son could know, and only a son could tell. It was a heartwarming and uplifting occasion.

This remarkable passage in Matthew shows Jesus coming to the same recognition about the one he called 'father'. There were things about his father that, for some reason, only he seemed to know, and only he could tell.

There is a deep mystery here which takes us right to the heart of what it meant to be Jesus. As he announced God's kingdom and put God's powerful love to work in healing, forgiving and bringing new life, he obviously realized that the other people he met, including the religious leaders, his own followers, and the ordinary people, didn't have the same awareness of his father that he did.

Imagine a gifted musician walking around among people who can only just manage to sing in tune. That must have been what it was like for Jesus. He must have known from early on that there was something different about him, that he seemed to have an inside track on knowing who Israel's God truly was, and what he was wanting for his people.

This must have made it all the more galling when he discovered that most of his contemporaries didn't want to hear what he was telling them. Most of them, alarmed at the direct challenge he presented, were either resisting him outright or making excuses for not believing him or following him. Opposition was mounting. And, strangely, this gave Jesus a fresh, further insight into the way his father was operating. This, in turn, resulted in a burst of praise as he glimpsed the strange, unexpected way God was working.

Jewish writings had, for a millennium and more, spoken warmly about the wisdom of the wise. God gave wisdom to those who feared him; a long tradition of Torah-study and piety indicated that those who devoted themselves to learning the law and trying to tease out its finer points would become wise, would ultimately know God. For the average Jew of Jesus' day, this put 'wisdom' about as far out of reach as being a brain surgeon or test pilot seems for most people today. You needed to be a scholar, trained in languages and literature, with leisure to ponder and discuss weighty and complicated matters.

Jesus sliced through all that with a stroke. No, he declared: you just need to be a little child. Jesus had come to know his father the way a son does: not by studying books about him, but by living in his presence, listening for his voice, and learning from him as an apprentice does from a master, by watching and imitating. And he was now discovering that the wise and learned were getting nowhere, and that the 'little people' – the poor, the sinners, the tax-collectors, ordinary folk – were discovering more of God, simply by following him, Jesus, than the learned specialists who declared that what he was doing didn't fit with their complicated theories.

As a result, Jesus had come to see that he was himself acting as a window onto the living God. Where he was, and through his words, people were coming to see who 'the father' really was. He seemed to have the gift and the task of drawing back the curtain and 'unveiling' the truth about God; and the word for 'unveil' here is *apocalypse*, which still today speaks of something dramatic, sudden and earth-shattering.

Wasn't that a bit daunting for his followers? Isn't it rather forbidding to discover that the true God can be known only through Jesus? No. It might have felt like that if it had been somebody else; but with Jesus everything was different. It gave him the platform from which to issue what is still the most welcoming and encouraging invitation ever offered. 'Come to me,' he said, 'and I'll give you rest.' This is the invitation which pulls back the curtain and lets us see who 'the father' really is – and encourages us to come into his loving, welcoming presence.

For reflection or discussion

- The passage suggests that the wisdom and learning of scholars and experts may not necessarily lead to a deeper knowledge of God. In what ways can your own preconceived notions, intellectual pursuits or religious traditions hinder you from truly encountering God's presence? How can you cultivate a childlike openness and receptivity to knowing and following God?
- Jesus invites people to 'come to me' as a welcoming and encouraging offer of rest. What does it mean to find rest in the knowledge and understanding of God through Jesus?

Wednesday

Glorify the son: John 17.1–8

[1]After Jesus had said this, he lifted up his eyes to heaven.

'Father,' he said, 'the moment has come. Glorify your son, so that your son may glorify you. ²Do this in the same way as you did when you gave him authority over all flesh, so that he could give the life of God's coming age to everyone you gave him. ³And by "the life of God's coming age" I mean this: that they should know you, the only true God, and Jesus the Messiah, the one you sent.

⁴'I glorified you on earth, by completing the work you gave me to do. ⁵So now, father, glorify me, alongside yourself, with the glory which I had with you before the world existed.

⁶'I revealed your name to the people you gave me out of the world. They belonged to you; you gave them to me; and they have kept your word. ⁷Now they know that everything which you gave me comes from you. ⁸I have given them the words you gave me, and they have received them. They have come to know, in truth, that I came from you. They have believed that you sent me.'

Shakespeare's play *Hamlet* is full of action. Ghosts, murders, love scenes, plots, accidental killings, betrayals, recriminations and more plots. The play highlights the indecision of the hero when faced with huge problems, and this results in pauses here and there. But at one moment in particular the action comes to a shuddering halt. Hamlet is looking for an opportunity to take revenge on his stepfather, Claudius, for murdering his father and usurping the throne of Denmark. He comes upon an ideal opportunity: Claudius is in his chamber, kneeling quietly. But Hamlet stops, and thinks. Claudius is praying! If he takes revenge now, Claudius may perhaps have repented and will be saved. Hamlet decides to wait for a better moment. The sorry tale continues.

He is praying! There is a mystery there which nobody can penetrate except the one who is doing the praying. Just as I cannot be sure that when you see something red you are seeing exactly the same colour as I am, so I cannot be sure what passes between you and God when you kneel down and pray. Hamlet couldn't tell what Claudius was praying, but knew he should pause and wait. And, with a totally different king, equally caught up in mystery, intrigue and plots but innocent of all, we come to a place where we, too, should pause and wait, and perhaps quietly join in.

Jesus is praying! Of course, we know that Jesus prayed. The gospels tell us that frequently. But they hardly ever tell us what he prayed or how he prayed. A few sentences at most come down to us, such as that wonderful passage in Matthew (11.25–27), and the burst of praise at the tomb of Lazarus (John 11.41–42). Interestingly, both of those passages look remarkably like shorter versions of what we find in this outstanding, ecstatic chapter in the Gospel of John. I once heard an actor read the whole of John's gospel, and when he came to this chapter he knelt down and prayed it as a prayer. It sounded, and *felt*, like prayer. This is not simply a theological treatise, with John putting ideas together and placing them on Jesus' lips.

Nor, we may suppose, is John remembering it all without having prayed through it himself, over and over again. The mention of 'Jesus the Messiah' in verse 3 sounds very strange from Jesus himself; perhaps here, and maybe elsewhere too, John the praying teacher, in order to make the prayer his own and pass it on to his own followers, has turned phrases round so that they become (so to speak) prayable by the continuing community. But in essence the prayer draws together everything that the gospel story has been about up to this point.

I remember the first time, as a young musician, that I sat in the middle of a school orchestra and played my small part with the music *happening all round me*, instead of coming at me from the loudspeaker of a radio or record player. When you make this prayer your own, when you enter into this chapter and see what happens, you are being invited to come into the heart of that intimate relation between Jesus and the father and have it, so to speak, happen all round you. That is both what the prayer embodies and also its central subject matter.

This first section of the prayer is a celebration and a request. The two are closely linked. Jesus is celebrating the fact that his work is done. Yes, there is the huge and awful task awaiting him the next day. But he has completed the deeds and words which the father gave him to do. (Those who see Jesus as simply a great teacher, or think that his task was to heal as many as possible, naturally find this a puzzle.) He has laid before his chosen disciples all that the father has given to him. That is the reason for the celebration, and it is the ground of the request he now makes.

His request is that he may now be exalted, glorified, lifted up to that position alongside the father which in Jewish tradition the king, the Messiah, the son of man, was supposed to attain. The Messiah, say the psalms, will rule a kingdom that stretches from sea to sea, from 'the River' to 'the ends of the earth' (Psalm 72.8). In other words, he will have a universal dominion. 'One like a son of man' will be exalted to share the throne of God himself (Daniel 7).

When the Messiah takes his seat, exalted over the world, then the age to come will truly have begun – that 'coming age' which Jewish prophets longed for, which Jewish sages taught would appear at the end of 'the present age'. It would be the time of new life, life with a new quality (not just quantity, going on and on for ever). It would be, in our inadequate phrase, 'eternal life'.

This 'eternal life', this life of the coming age, is not just something people can have after their death. It isn't simply that in some future state the world will go on for ever and ever and we shall be part of it. The point is, rather, that this new sort of life has come to birth in the world in and through Jesus. Once he has completed the final victory over death itself, all his followers, all who trust him and believe that he has truly come from the father, and has truly unveiled the father's character and purpose – all of them can and will possess 'eternal life' right here and now. That, too, is one of the great themes of this gospel (e.g. 3.16; 5.24).

So far, the prayer may seem far too exalted for us to join in. But, as we shall see in the next two sections, the relationship between Jesus and the father, though it seems extraordinarily close and trusting, is not designed to be exclusive. We are invited to join in.

For reflection or discussion

- How can you cultivate a sense of closeness and communion with God in your life? What practices or attitudes can help us to experience the presence of God 'happening all around us'?
- How does the understanding of eternal life in the Gospel of John differ from common conceptions of life after death? How does this understanding shape your own concept of the present moment and your relationship with God?

Thursday

Jesus prays for his people: John 17.9–19

[9]'I'm praying for them. I'm not praying for the world, but for the people you've given me. They belong to you. [10]All mine are yours; all yours are mine; and I'm glorified in them.

[11]'I'm not in the world any longer, but they're still in the world; I'm coming to you. Holy father, keep them in your name, the name you've given to me, so that they may be one, just as we are one.

[12]'When I was with them, I kept them in your name, the name you've given me. I guarded them, and none of them has been destroyed (except the son of destruction; that's what the Bible said would happen). [13]But now I'm coming to you. I'm speaking these things in the world, so that they can have my joy fulfilled in them.

[14]'I have given them your word. The world hated them, because they are not from the world, just as I am not from the world. [15]I'm not asking that you should take them out of the world, but that you should keep them from the evil

one. [16]They didn't come from the world, just as I didn't come from the world. [17]Set them apart for yourself in the truth; your word is truth. [18]Just as you sent me into the world, so I sent them into the world. [19]And on their account I set myself apart for you, so that they, too, may be set apart for you in the truth.'

In the newspapers recently a mother was punished by the courts. She had left her two young children entirely by themselves, while she went off for a foreign holiday with her new boyfriend. (The father, it seems, was nowhere to be found.) It is hard to believe that a mother could do such a thing. One wonders what she thought she would find when she got home. Tragically, such things happen in our world today.

But supposing she herself had had loving parents who were only too glad to look after the children while she was away. That would have made all the difference. She could have entrusted the little ones to them, safe in the knowledge that they would care for them as much as she did. One can imagine a mother in that situation giving her parents detailed instructions as to how each child should be looked after, not because she didn't trust her parents to look after them but because she did.

What Jesus now prays grows out of the fact that he is going away. He is entrusting the disciples to the father he has known and loved throughout his own earthly life, the father who, he knows, will care for them every bit as much as he has done himself. He is very much aware that the disciples are at risk. The world, which hates them as it hated him, will threaten and abuse them. They don't belong to it, but they are to be sent into it, and they need protecting. That's what the prayer is about.

This section begins with a description of who Jesus' followers are. They are the ones the father has given to Jesus; they already belong to him, and Jesus is handing them back into his safe keeping.

They are distinct from 'the world'. Insofar as they are the new, cleansed people they have become through Jesus' call and teaching, they are not 'from the world'.

This can seem puzzling, and we'd better explain it a bit more. Jesus is not suggesting that his followers don't possess human ancestry, homes and families, and physical bodies which will one day decay and die. 'The world' in this gospel doesn't mean simply the physical universe as we know it. It means the world insofar as it has rebelled against God, has chosen darkness rather than light, and has organized itself to oppose the creator. Seen from within that 'world', Jesus is 'from' elsewhere. So too, we now discover to our surprise, are the disciples. In other words, 'the world' in this dark sense is not the place, the force, the sphere, that determines who the disciples most truly are.

What they now need, therefore, is to be kept from being pulled back into 'the world' with all its wickedness and rebellion. During his public ministry, teaching them and leading them, Jesus has looked after them, like the shepherd with his sheep. Now, because he is coming to the father, he is entrusting them to the father, who will continue the work of keeping them safe.

He therefore addresses the father as 'holy' (verse 11), and declares that he is 'setting himself apart' so that the disciples too may be 'set apart'. The word for 'setting apart' is basically the same as the word for 'holy'; but our word 'holy', when applied to people, can give a sense of over-pious religiosity which is foreign to the New Testament. What is 'holiness' in Jesus' world?

In first-century Judaism, 'holiness' called to mind the Temple in particular. It was the holy place, the place where the holy God had promised to live. It referred particularly to the Holy of Holies, the innermost shrine, where the high priest would go once a year to make atonement for the people. The high priest had to go through special ceremonies of 'consecration', to be 'set apart' so that he could enter into the presence of the holy God, and pray there for his people.

In exactly the same way, Jesus is declaring that he has been, all along, 'set apart', 'consecrated' for God's exclusive service. Now, like the high priest, he is asking the father to preserve his people from evil, from the tricks and traps of 'the world'. He wants them to be his holy people in the best and fullest sense.

What Jesus has already done for them is to 'keep' them in the father's name (verse 12) and to give them his word (verse 14). In other words, when he now entrusts them to the father, this won't mean a sudden change, like a mother entrusting her children to someone of whom they've never heard and whose house will be run on quite different lines from their own home. He has already taught them, so to speak, the table manners appropriate for the father's house. In praying for them now, he is simply praying that what he has begun, the father will gloriously complete.

This prayer has been used for many centuries by pastors, teachers and other Christian leaders as they pray for those in their care. It can also, with only slight variation, be used by Christians of all sorts for themselves. Substitute 'Jesus' where the prayer says 'I', and replace 'they' and 'them' with 'I' and 'me', and you'll get the idea. But be careful. This is a serious prayer. It is one of the most serious things Jesus ever said. That's why, deep down, it is also among the most joyful and hopeful. Pray it with awe, and with delight.

For reflection or discussion

- In what ways do you resonate with the idea of being 'in the world, but not of the world'? How do you navigate the tension between belonging to a broken world and being called to live as a follower of Jesus?
- Consider the concept of being 'set apart' or 'holy' as described in the passage. How does this understanding challenge common perceptions of holiness? How can you cultivate a sense of being set apart for God's service in your daily life?

Friday

That they may be one: John 17.20–26

[20]'I'm not praying simply for them. I'm praying, too, for the people who will come to believe in me because of their word. [21]I am praying that they may all be one – just as you, father, are in me, and I in you, that they too may be in us, so that the world may believe that you sent me.

[22]'I have given them the glory which you have given to me, so that they may be one, just as we are one. [23]I in them, and you in me; yes, they must be completely one, so that the world may know that you sent me, and that you loved them just as you loved me.

[24]'Father, I want the ones you've given me to be with me where I am. I want them to see my glory, the glory which you've given me, because you loved me before the foundation of the world.

[25]'Righteous father, even the world didn't know you. But I have known you, and these ones have known that you sent me. [26]I made your name known to them – yes, and I will make it known; so that the love with which you loved me may be in them, and I in them.'

Imagine some great figure of the past. Shakespeare, perhaps. George Washington, possibly. Socrates. Think of someone you respect and admire. Now imagine that the historians have just found, among old manuscripts, a letter from the great man himself. And imagine that it was talking about . . . you. How would you feel?

That is how you should feel as you read verse 20. Jesus is talking about *you*. And me. 'Those who believe in me through their word'; that is, through the word of his followers. His followers announced the message around the world. Those who heard them passed it on.

And on, and on, and on. The church is never more than one generation away from extinction; all it would take is for a single generation
not to hand the word on. But it's never happened. People have always
told other people. I am writing this book, and you are reading it, as a
result. It's awesome, when you come to think about it.

But what is Jesus praying for, as he thinks about you and me and
all his other followers in this and every generation? He is praying
that we may be, just as the old words say, 'one, holy and universal',
founded on the teaching of the followers, the 'apostles', the ones who
were with him on that occasion. In particular, he longed that we
should all be one. United.

This unity isn't to be just a formal arrangement. It isn't just an
outward thing. It is based on, and must mirror, nothing less than
the unity between the father and the son. Just as the father is in the
son, and the son in the father, so we too are to live within that unity.
That can only mean that we ourselves are to be united. And, in case
we might miss the point, the result of this will be that the world will
see, and know, that this kind of human community, united across
all traditional barriers of race, custom, gender or class, can only come
from the action of the creator God. 'So that the world may believe . . .'

Notice how this picks up what Jesus said in 13.35. 'This is how all
people will know that you are my disciples: if you have love for each
other.' Unity is vital. Often we sense it, heard like soft music through the
partition walls we set up around ourselves. Sometimes we experience
it, when for a moment we meet Christians from a totally different
background and discover that, despite our many differences, and the
traditions that keep us apart, we know a unity of love and devotion that
cannot be broken. But just as often, alas, we experience, sense and know
that Jesus' prayer for us has not yet been fully answered.

As in any human relationship, unity cannot be forced. There can
be no bullying, no manipulation. But in a divided world, where the divisions have often run down so-called 'religious' lines, there is no ex-
cuse for Christians not to work afresh in every generation towards the

unity Jesus prayed for. If we are, essentially, one in faith, there can be no final reason why we may not be one, also, in our life and worship. In addition, Jesus returns to an earlier theme (see 12.26 and 14.3). His followers are to be 'with him', to see his glory. They are to know and experience the fact that the father has exalted him as the sovereign of the world. They are to know that the love which the creator God has given to him has installed him as the loving Lord of all.

Many Christians today draw back from that statement. They suppose, naturally enough, that it will sound arrogant, or as though they are giving themselves a special status by claiming this about Jesus. But this is to misunderstand the whole message of the gospel. When Jesus is exalted, the reason is nothing other than love. This is not the sort of sovereignty that enables people to think themselves better than others. It is the sort of sovereignty that commits them, as it committed Jesus, to loving service.

That's what the whole prayer comes down to in the end (verse 26). It is about the love of the father surrounding Jesus, and this same love, as a bond and badge, surrounding all Jesus' people, making him present to them and through them to the world. And, whereas in verse 11 Jesus addressed the father as 'holy', now he addresses him as 'righteous' (verse 25). The father is the judge of all the earth; though the world rages against Jesus' followers, he will see that right will prevail.

But, as always in the New Testament, the justice for which we pray, the righteous judgment through which the father expresses himself in his world, appears before us as love. That is because, supremely, it appears before us in the person of Jesus: this Jesus, this man who prayed for you and me, this high priest who set himself apart for the father's glad service.

For reflection or discussion

- How does it make you feel to know that Jesus prayed for his followers throughout history, including you? What does this reveal about the impact of the message passed down by Jesus' followers?

- How does Jesus' sovereignty, rooted in love, challenge common notions of power and authority? In what ways can you emulate Jesus' example of loving service in your own life?

Saturday

Gethsemane: Matthew 26.36–46

[36]So Jesus went with them to the place called Gethsemane.

'You sit here,' he said to the disciples, 'while I go over there and pray.'

[37]He took Peter and the two sons of Zebedee with him, and began to be very upset and distressed.

[38]'My soul is overwhelmed with grief,' he said, 'even to death. Stay here and keep watch with me.'

[39]Then, going a little further on, he fell on his face and prayed.

'My father,' he said, 'if it's possible – please, please let this cup go away from me! But . . . not what I want, but what you want.'

[40]He came back to the disciples and found them asleep.

'So,' he said to Peter, 'couldn't you keep watch with me for a single hour? [41]Watch and pray so that you don't get pulled down into the time of testing. The spirit is eager, but the body is weak.'

[42]Again, for the second time, he went off and said, 'My father, if it's not possible for this to pass unless I drink it, let your will be done.'

[43]Again he came and found them asleep; their eyes were heavy. [44]Once more he left them and went away. He prayed for the third time, using the same words once again. [45]Then he came back to the disciples.

'You can sleep now,' he said, 'and have a good rest! Look – the time has come, and the son of man is given over into the hands of wicked people! [46]Get up and let's be going. Look! Here comes the one who's going to betray me!'

There was once a small girl who had never seen her father anything but cheerful. As long as she could remember, he seemed to have been smiling at her. He had smiled when she was born, the daughter he had longed for. He had smiled as he held her in his arms and helped her to learn to eat and drink. He had laughed as he played with her, encouraged her with games and toys as she learned to walk, chatted brightly as he took her to school. If she hurt herself, his smile and gentle kiss helped her to relax and get over it. If she was in difficulties or trouble, the shadow that would cross his face was like a small cloud which hardly succeeded in hiding the sun; soon the smile would come out again, the eager interest in some new project, something to distract, to move on to new worlds.

And then one day it happened.

To begin with she wasn't told why. He came back home from a visit, and with a look she'd never seen before went straight to his room. Ever afterwards she would remember the sounds she then heard, the sounds she never thought to hear.

The sound of a healthy, strapping thirty-year-old man weeping for a dead sister.

It was of course a necessary part of growing up. In most families, grief would have struck sooner. Looking back, she remained grateful for the years when smiles and laughter were all she could remember. But the shock of his sudden vulnerability, far more than the fact of the death of her aunt and all that it meant, were what made the deepest impression.

I think Gethsemane was the equivalent moment for the disciples.

Oh, Jesus had been sad at various times. He'd been frustrated with them for not understanding what he was talking about. He'd been cross with the people who were attacking him, misunderstanding him, accusing him of all sorts of ridiculous things. There had even been tension with his own family. But basically he'd always been the strong one. Always ready with another story, another sharp one-liner to turn the tables on some probing questioner, another soaring vision of God and the kingdom. It was always they who had the problems, he who had the answers.

And now this.

Jesus was like a man in a waking nightmare. He could see, as though it was before his very eyes, the cup. Not the cup he had spoken of, and given them to drink, in the intense and exciting atmosphere of the Last Supper an hour or so before. This was the cup he had mentioned to James and John (20.22–23), the cup the prophets had spoken of. The cup of God's wrath.

He didn't want to drink it. He badly didn't want to. Jesus at this point was no hero-figure, marching boldly towards his oncoming fate. He was no Socrates, drinking the poison and telling his friends to stop crying because he was going to a much better life. He was a man, as we might say, in melt-down mode. He had looked into the darkness and seen the grinning faces of all the demons in the world looking back at him. And he begged and begged his father not to bring him to the point of going through with it. He prayed the prayer he had taught them to pray: Don't let us be brought into the time of testing, the time of deepest trial!

And the answer was a refusal.

Actually, we can see the answer being given, more subtly than that implies, as the first frantic and panicky prayer turns into the second and then the third. To begin with, a straight request ('Let the cup pass me by'), with a sad recognition that God has the right to say no if that's the way it has to be. Then, a prayer which echoes another phrase in the Lord's Prayer: if it has to be, 'may your will be done'. The disciples probably didn't realize that, when Jesus gave them the Lord's Prayer (6.9–13), this much of it would be so directly relevant to him. He had to live what he taught. Indeed, the whole Sermon on the Mount seemed to be coming true in him, as he himself faced the suffering and sorrow of which he'd spoken, on his way to being struck on the cheek, to being cursed and responding with blessings. Here, for the second time in the gospel narrative (the first time being the temptation story in 4.1–11), we see Jesus fighting in private the spiritual battle he needed to win if he was then to stand in public and speak, and live, and die for God's kingdom.

The shocking lesson for the disciples can, of course, be turned to excellent use if we learn, in our own prayer, to wait with them, to keep awake and watch with Jesus. At any given moment, someone we know is facing darkness and horror: illness, death, bereavement, torture, catastrophe, loss. They ask us, perhaps silently, to stay with them, to watch and pray alongside them.

Distance is no object. In any one day we may be called to kneel in Gethsemane beside someone dying in a hospital in Nairobi, someone being tortured for their faith in Myanmar, someone who has lost a job in New York, someone else waiting anxiously for a doctor's report in Edinburgh. Once we ourselves get over the shock of realizing that all our friends, neighbours and family, and even the people we have come to rely on, are themselves vulnerable and need our support – if even Jesus longed for his friends' support, how much more should we! – we should be prepared to give it to the fullest of our ability.

And when we ourselves find the ground giving way beneath our feet, as sooner or later we shall, Gethsemane is where to go. That is where we find that the Lord of the world, the one to whom is now committed all authority (28.18), has been there before us.

For reflection or discussion

- Consider the significance of Jesus' prayer in relation to the Lord's Prayer. How does Jesus' personal experience in Gethsemane align with the prayer he taught his disciples? In what ways can you apply the principles of the Lord's Prayer in your own life, particularly during times of darkness and trial?
- Reflect on the meaning of empathy and the need to support others in their moments of darkness and horror. How can you practically demonstrate solidarity and compassion towards

those facing illness, loss or persecution? What role does prayer and emotional presence play in supporting others through their challenges?

Week 3
Jesus among friends

Monday

The death of Lazarus: John 11.1–16

¹There was a man in Bethany named Lazarus, and he became ill. Bethany was the village of Mary and her sister Martha. (²This was the Mary who anointed the Lord with myrrh, and wiped his feet with her hair. Lazarus, who was ill, was her brother.)

³So the sisters sent messengers to Jesus.

'Master,' they said, 'the man you love is ill.'

⁴When Jesus got the message, he said, 'This illness won't lead to death. It's all about the glory of God! The son of God will be glorified through it.'

⁵Now Jesus loved Martha, and her sister, and Lazarus. ⁶So when he heard that he was ill, he stayed where he was for two days.

⁷Then, after that, he said to the disciples, 'Let's go back to Judaea.'

⁸'Teacher,' replied the disciples, 'the Judaeans were trying to stone you just now! Surely you don't want to go back *there*!'

⁹'There are twelve hours in the day, aren't there?' replied Jesus. 'If you walk in the day, you won't trip up, because you'll see the light of this world. ¹⁰But if anyone walks in the night, they will trip up, because there is no light in them.'

¹¹When he had said this, Jesus added: 'Our friend Lazarus has fallen asleep. But I'm going to wake him up.'

[12]'Master,' replied the disciples, 'if he's asleep, he'll be all right.'

([13]They thought he was referring to ordinary sleep; but Jesus had in fact been speaking of his death.)

[14]Then Jesus spoke to them plainly.

'Lazarus', he said, 'is dead. [15]Actually, I'm glad I wasn't there, for your sakes; it will help your faith. But let's go to him.'

[16]Thomas, whose name was the Twin, addressed the other disciples.

'Let's go too,' he said. 'We may as well die with him.'

Why didn't they *do* something?

A friend of mine had been invited to take on the leadership of a vibrant, growing church. He and his family were eager to go and meet this new challenge. But the church authorities seemed to be dragging their feet about where he was going to live. The present house was quite unsuitable; should they build a new one? Should they convert an existing church building? Should they house him some way off for the time being and hope something would turn up?

Meanwhile suitable houses, near the church, were coming on the market, and nothing was being done. My friend and his family prayed about it, and still nothing happened. I and others prayed about it, wrote letters, made phone calls, and still nothing happened. The time came for him to be installed at the church; it was a great occasion, but still nothing definite had happened. Finally, as the whole church prayed about what was to be done, the log-jam burst. The decision was made. And one of the most suitable houses, which they had looked at from the beginning, had now come down in price. The church authorities bought it, the family moved in and the new ministry began.

But I shan't forget the months of frustration, during which it seemed as though nothing was happening. It seemed as though God was ignoring our prayers for the proper solution. We all got tired of it. People became irritable and wondered if we'd made some mistake somewhere. And I know that there are many stories like that which don't have a happy ending at all, or not yet. In many ways the story of the world is like that. We pray for justice and peace, for prosperity and harmony between nations and races. And still it hasn't happened.

God doesn't play games with us. Of that I am quite sure. And yet his ways are not our ways. His timing is not our timing. One of the most striking reminders of this is in verse 6 of the present passage. When Jesus got the message from the two sisters, the cry for help, the emergency-come-quickly appeal, *he stayed where he was for two days.* He didn't even mention it to the disciples. He didn't make preparations to go. He didn't send messages back to say 'We're on our way'. He just stayed there. And Mary and Martha, in Bethany, watched their beloved brother die.

What was Jesus doing? From the rest of the story, I think we can tell. He was praying. He was wrestling with the father's will. The disciples were quite right (verse 8): the Judaeans had been wanting to stone him, and surely he wouldn't think of going back just yet? Bethany was and is a small town just two miles or so from Jerusalem, on the eastern slopes of the Mount of Olives. Once you're there, you're within easy reach of the holy city. And who knew what would happen this time?

It's important to realize that this wonderful story about Lazarus, one of the most powerful and moving in the whole Bible, is not just about Lazarus. It's also about Jesus. The chapter begins with the disciples warning Jesus not to go back to Judaea; it ends with the high priest declaring that one man must die for the people (verse 50). And when Jesus thanks the father that he has heard his prayer (verses 41–42), I think he's referring to the prayers he prayed during those two strange, silent days in the wilderness across the Jordan (10.40). He was praying for Lazarus, but he was also praying for wisdom and guidance as to his own plans and movements.

Somehow the two were bound up together. What Jesus was going to do for Lazarus would be, on the one hand, a principal reason why the authorities would want him out of the way (verses 45–53). But on the other hand, it would be the most powerful sign yet of what Jesus' life and work was all about, and of how in particular it would reach its climactic resolution.

The time of waiting, therefore, was vital. As so often, Jesus needed to be in prayer, exploring the father's will in that intimacy and union of which he often spoke. Only then would he act – not in the way Mary and Martha had wanted him to do, but in a manner beyond their wildest dreams.

The word 'Beth-any' means, literally, 'the house of the poor'. There is some evidence that it was just that: a place where poor, needy and sick people could be cared for, a kind of hospice a little way outside the city. Jesus had been there before, perhaps several times. He may have had a special affection for the place, and it for him, as he demonstrated again and again his own care for those in need, and assured them of the promise of the kingdom in which the poor would celebrate and the sick be healed. John points us on, in verse 2, to the moment which he will later describe (12.1–8), when Mary poured expensive perfume on Jesus' feet and provoked a fuss about why it hadn't been given to the poor. Extravagance doesn't go down well in a poor-house.

But this story is all about the ways in which Jesus surprises people and overturns their expectations. He didn't go when the sisters asked him. He did eventually go, although the disciples warned him not to. He spoke about 'sleep', meaning death, and the disciples thought he meant ordinary sleep. And, in the middle (verse 9), he told them in a strange little saying that people who walk in the daytime don't trip up, but people who walk around in the darkness do. What did he mean?

He seems to have meant that the only way to know where you are going is to follow him. If you try to steer your course by your own understanding, you'll trip up, because you'll be in the dark. But if you stick close to him, and see the situation from his point of view, then, even if it means days and perhaps years of puzzlement, wondering why nothing seems to be happening, you will come out at the right place in the end.

The end of the passage introduces us to one of John's great minor characters. Thomas is loyal, dogged, slow to understand things, but determined to go on putting one foot in front of another at Jesus' command. Now he speaks words heavy with foreboding for what's to come: 'Let's go too, and die with him.' They don't die with him, of course, or not yet, but this is certainly the right response. There is a great deal that we don't understand, and our hopes and plans often get thwarted. But if we go with Jesus, even if it's into the jaws of death, we will be walking in the light, whereas if we press ahead arrogantly with our own plans and ambitions we are bound to trip up.

For reflection or discussion

- Why did Jesus delay responding to Mary and Martha's cry for help? Do you ever find that God's timing doesn't match the hopes and expectations expressed in your prayers? How can you find patience and trust in God's plans even when they seem delayed, or different from your own desires?
- In what areas of your life do you struggle with relinquishing control and trusting in Jesus' leading? How can you cultivate a mindset of walking in the light and surrendering your plans to God's will?

Tuesday

The resurrection and the life: John 11.17–27

[17]When Jesus arrived, he found that Lazarus had already been in the tomb for four days. [18]Bethany was near Jerusalem, about

two miles away. [19]Many of the Judaeans had come to Martha and Mary to console them about their brother.

[20]When Martha heard that Jesus had arrived, she went to meet him. Mary, meanwhile, stayed sitting at home.

[21]'Master!' said Martha to Jesus. 'If only you'd been here! Then my brother wouldn't have died! [22]But even now I know that God will give you whatever you ask him.'

[23]'Your brother will rise again,' replied Jesus.

[24]'I know he'll rise again,' said Martha, 'in the resurrection on the last day.'

[25]'I am the resurrection and the life,' replied Jesus. 'Anyone who believes in me will live, even if they die. [26]And anyone who lives and believes in me will never, ever die. Do you believe this?'

[27]'Yes, Master,' she said. 'This is what I've come to believe: that you are the Messiah, the son of God, the one who was to come into the world.'

When did you last say 'If only . . .'?

If only he hadn't stepped out in front of that car . . .

If only she had worked a bit harder and not failed the exam . . .

If only a different president had been elected last time round . . .

If only we hadn't decided to go on holiday that very week . . .

And whatever it was, you will know the sickening sense of wanting to turn the clock back. That's why movies are made, like that *Back to the Future* series, in which people do just that, moving this way and that within the long history of time, changing something in a previous generation which will mean that now everything in the present – and the future – can be different. And of course it's a wistful dream. It's a kind of nostalgia, not for the past as it was, but for the present that could have been, *if only* the past had just been a little bit different. Like all nostalgia, it's a bitter-sweet feeling, caressing the moment that might have been, while knowing it's all fantasy.

All of that and more is here (verse 21) in Martha's 'if only' to Jesus. She knows that if Jesus had been there he would have cured Lazarus. And she probably knows, too, that it has taken Jesus at least two days longer to get there than she had hoped. Lazarus, as we discover later, has already been dead for three days, but perhaps . . . he might just have made it . . . if only . . .

Jesus' reply to her, and the conversation they then have, show that the 'back to the future' idea isn't entirely a movie-maker's fantasy. Instead of looking at the past, and dreaming about what might have been (but now can't be), he invites her to look to the future. Then, having looked to the future, he asks her to imagine that the future is suddenly brought forwards into the present. This, in fact, is central to all early Christian beliefs about Jesus, and the present passage makes the point as clearly and vividly as anywhere in the whole New Testament.

First, he points her to the future. 'Your brother will rise again.' She knows, as well as Jesus does, that this is standard Jewish teaching. (Some Jews, particularly the Sadducees, didn't believe in a future resurrection, but at this period most Jews did, following Daniel 12.3 and other key Old Testament passages.) They shared the vision of Isaiah 65 and 66: a vision of new heavens and new earth, God's whole new world, a world like ours only with its beauty and power enhanced and its pain, ugliness and grief abolished. Within that new world, they believed, all God's people from ancient times to the present would be given new bodies, to share and relish the life of the new creation.

Martha believes this, but her rather flat response in verse 24 shows that it isn't at the moment very comforting. But she isn't prepared for Jesus' response. The future has burst into the present. The new creation, and with it the resurrection, has come forward from the end of time into the middle of time. Jesus has not just come, as we sometimes say or sing, 'from heaven to earth'; it is equally true to say that he has come from God's future into the present, into the mess and muddle of the world we know. 'I am the resurrection and the life,' he says. 'Resurrection' isn't just a doctrine. It isn't just a future fact. It's a *person*, and here he is standing in front of Martha, teasing her to make the huge jump of trust and hope.

He is challenging her, urging her, to exchange her 'if only . . .' for an 'if Jesus . . .'.

If Jesus is who she is coming to believe he is . . .

If Jesus is the Messiah, the one who was promised by the prophets, the one who was to come into the world . . .

If he is God's own son, the one in whom the living God is strangely and newly present . . .

If he is resurrection-in-person, life-come-to-life . . .

The story breaks off at this point, keeping us in suspense while Martha goes to get her sister. But this suspense – John is, after all, a master storyteller – is designed not least to give us space to think the same questions through for ourselves. This is one of those stories in which it's not difficult to place ourselves among the characters.

Martha is the active, busy one (see Luke 10.38–42), and Mary the quieter. We shall see Mary's response presently. Martha had to hurry off to meet Jesus and confront him directly. Many of us are like that; we can't wait, we must tell Jesus what we think of him and his strange ways. If you're like that, and if you have an 'if only' in your heart or mind right now, put yourself in Martha's shoes. Run off to meet Jesus. Tell him the problem. Ask him why he didn't come sooner, why he allowed that awful thing to happen.

And then be prepared for a surprising response. I can't predict what the response will be, for the very good reason that it is always, always a surprise. But I do know the shape that it will take. Jesus will meet your problem with some new part of God's future that can and will burst into your present time, into the mess and grief, with good news, with hope, with new possibilities.

And the key to it all, now as then, is faith. Jesus is bringing God's new world to birth; but it doesn't happen automatically. It doesn't just sweep everyone along with it, willy-nilly. The key to sharing the new world is faith: believing in Jesus, trusting that he is God's Messiah, the one coming into the world, into our world, into our pain and sorrow and death.

For reflection or discussion

- What did Jesus mean by declaring he is 'the resurrection and the life'? How does Jesus bring God's future into the present? How does this understanding of Jesus challenge our conventional notions of time and the limitations of our circumstances?
- Consider your own response to trials and disappointments. Are you more like Martha, taking immediate action and seeking direct confrontation, or like Mary, adopting a quieter and more contemplative approach? Reflect on how you typically approach Jesus with your concerns and questions. How can you open yourself to being surprised by Jesus' response and allowing him to bring new possibilities and hope into your life?

Wednesday

Jesus goes to the tomb: John 11.28–37

²⁸Martha went back and called her sister Mary.

'The teacher has come,' she said to her privately, 'and he's asking for you.'

²⁹When she heard that, she got up quickly and went to him. ³⁰Jesus hadn't yet arrived in the village. He was still in the place where Martha had met him.

³¹The Judaeans who were in the house with Mary, consoling her, saw her get up quickly and go out. They guessed that she was going to the tomb to weep there, and they followed her.

³²When Mary came to where Jesus was, she saw him and fell down at his feet.

'Master!' she said. 'If only you'd been here, my brother wouldn't have died!'

³³When Jesus saw her crying, and the Judaeans who had come with her crying, he was deeply stirred in his spirit, and very troubled.

³⁴'Where have you laid him?' he asked.

'Master,' they said, 'come and see.'

³⁵Jesus burst into tears.

³⁶'Look,' said the Judaeans, 'see how much he loved him!'

³⁷'Well, yes,' some of them said, 'but he opened the eyes of a blind man, didn't he? Couldn't he have done something to stop this fellow from dying?'

One of the greatest cultural divides in today's world is the different ways in which we do funerals.

In many parts of the world people still mourn their dead in much the same way that they did in Jesus' day. There are processions, carrying the coffin along the streets to the place of burial or cremation. Everyone, particularly the women, cries and wails. There is wild, sad music. The process of grief is well and truly launched. One person's grief communicates to another; it's part of the strange business of being human that when we are with very sad people their sadness infects us even if we don't share their particular grief. (The psychologists would point out that we all carry deep griefs of one sort or another, and these come to the surface when we are with others who have more immediate reason for sorrow.)

In other cultures, not least in the secularized world of the modern West, we have learned to hide our emotions. I well remember visiting an old lady whose husband had died after more than forty years of marriage. She was busying herself with arrangements, making phone calls, sorting out clothes, wondering what she should wear at the funeral. On the day itself she was bright and perky, putting on a good show for her family and friends. She was with us as we went for a cup of tea afterwards, chatting cheerfully, not wanting anyone else to be upset. I couldn't help feeling that the older way, the way of most of the world to this day, is actually kinder. It doesn't do any good to hide grief, or pretend it doesn't exist.

When Paul says he doesn't want us to grieve like people who have no hope (1 Thessalonians 4.13) he doesn't mean that he doesn't want us to grieve at all; he means that there are two sorts of grief, a hopeless grief and a hopeful grief. Hopeful grief is still grief. It can still be very, very bitter.

As though to rub this point in, we find Jesus in this passage bursting into tears (verse 35). It's one of the most remarkable moments in the whole gospel story. There can be no doubt of its historical truth. Nobody in the early church, venerating Jesus and celebrating his own victory over death, would have invented such a thing. But we shouldn't miss the levels of meaning that John intends us to see within it.

To begin with, we should not rest content, as some older writers did, with treating Jesus' tears as evidence that he was a real human being, not just a divine being 'playing' at being human. That is no doubt true; but nobody in Jesus' world imagined he was anything other than a real, flesh-and-blood human being, with emotions like everyone else's.

Rather, throughout the gospel John is telling us something much more striking; that when we look at Jesus, *not least when we look at Jesus in tears*, we are seeing not just a flesh-and-blood human being but the Word made flesh (1.1–14). The Word, through whom the worlds were made, weeps like a baby at the grave of his friend. Only when we stop and ponder this will we understand the full mystery of John's gospel. Only when we put away our high-and-dry pictures of who God is and replace them with pictures in which the Word who is God can cry with the world's crying will we discover what the word 'God' really means.

Jesus bursts into tears the moment he sees Mary, and all the Judaeans with her, in tears. 'He has borne our griefs', said the prophet, 'and carried our sorrows' (Isaiah 53.4). Jesus doesn't sweep into the scene (as we might have supposed, and as later Christians inventing such a story would almost certainly have told us) and declare that tears are beside the point, that Lazarus is not dead, only asleep (see Mark 5.39). Even though, as his actions and words will shortly make clear, Jesus has no doubt what he will do, and what his father will do through him, there is no sense of triumphalism, of someone coming in smugly with the secret formula that will show how clever he is. There is, rather, the man of sorrows, acquainted with our grief and pain, sharing and bearing it to the point of tears.

What grief within Jesus' own heart was stirred by the tears of Mary and the crowd? We can only guess. But among those guesses we must place, not a grief for other deaths in the past, but a grief for a death still to come: his own. This passage points us forward to the questions that will be asked at Jesus' own death. Couldn't the man who did so many signs have brought it about that he himself didn't have to die? Couldn't the one who saved so many have in the end saved himself? John is telling us the answer by a thousand hints and images throughout his book. It is only *through* his death, it is only *through* his own sharing of the common fate of humanity, that the world can be saved. There is a line straight on from Jesus' tears in verse 35 to the death in which Jesus will share not only the grief, but also the doom of the world.

But there is also a hint of what will then follow. 'Where have you laid him?' Jesus asks Mary and the others. 'They have taken away my master,' says Mary Magdalene just a week or two later, 'and I don't know where they have laid him' (20.13). Listen to the echoes between the story of Lazarus and that of Jesus himself. That's part of the reason John has told the story at all. (The other gospels don't have it; some have suggested that they were anxious to protect Lazarus from the sort of unwelcome attention indicated in 12.9–11. Presumably this danger was past by the time John was writing.)

'Come and see,' they respond, as Jesus had responded to the early disciples' enquiry as to where he was staying (1.46). It is the simplest of invitations, and yet it goes to the heart of Christian faith. 'Come and see,' we say to Jesus, as we lead him, all tears, to the place of our deepest grief and sorrow. 'Come and see,' he says to us in reply, as he leads us through the sorrow to the place where he now dwells in light and love and resurrection glory.

For reflection or discussion

- Consider the significance of Jesus shedding tears at the grave of Lazarus. How does this moment reveal the depth of Jesus' humanity and his identification with human suffering?
- Why was it important for Jesus, the Word made flesh, to experience and share in our grief and pain? How does this shape your understanding of God's character and his presence in times of sorrow?

Thursday

The raising of Lazarus: John 11.38–46

[38]Jesus was once again deeply troubled within himself. He came to the tomb. It was a cave, and a stone was placed in front of it.

[39]'Take away the stone,' said Jesus.

'But, Master,' said Martha, the dead man's sister, 'there'll be a smell! It's the fourth day already!'

[40]'Didn't I tell you', said Jesus, 'that if you believed you would see God's glory?'

[41]So they took the stone away. Jesus lifted up his eyes.

'Thank you, father,' he said, 'for hearing me! [42]I know you always hear me, but I've said this because of the crowd standing around, so that they may believe that you sent me.'

[43]With these words, he gave a loud shout: 'Lazarus – come out!'

[44]And the dead man came out. He was tied up, hand and foot, with strips of linen, and his face was wrapped in a cloth.

'Untie him,' said Jesus, 'and let him go.'

[45]The result of all this was that several of the Judaeans who had come to Mary, and who had seen what he had done, believed in him. [46]But some of them went off to the Pharisees and told them what Jesus had done.

We saw a programme on the television last night about the fossilized remains of what looks like an ancient race of creatures. They seem to be like humans, but much taller. They appear to have been significantly different from any monkeys or apes known to us. Now the archaeologists are teaming up with explorers (all this taking place in some of the remotest mountains of China) to see if these creatures might still exist.

It's an exciting story, and a remarkable prospect. But I am fascinated by the way in which the archaeologists piece together their finds. Here is a fossil which seems to be part of an animal. Here is a bone which might be part of the same animal. Here is a piece of hair, stuck to a rock deep inside a cave, high in the mountains. Could they all go together? Could one of these puzzles explain the others?

The present passage is one of the most dramatic moments in the whole story of Jesus. When Jesus raised Jairus' daughter, he ordered almost everyone out of the room, and when it was over he told them not to tell anyone. Now he stands in front of a large crowd, puts his reputation on the line, and shouts to Lazarus to come out. (The tomb, like many at the time, was clearly a cave, with a large stone across its mouth.)

And the dead man comes out – a heart-stopping moment of shuddering horror and overwhelming joy, mixed together like dark mud and liquid gold. All this is hugely important. If we don't feel its power, and find ourselves driven to awe and thanks and hope, then either we haven't learned to read or we have hearts of stone.

There must have been many other newly buried people Jesus didn't attempt to raise. There is a mystery about this moment which is bound up with the mysterious uniqueness of Jesus' own work. He brought God's love and power into sharp and clear focus in one small place; only then would it go out into the rest of the world. This passage raises these questions for us quite sharply.

But the raising of Lazarus isn't itself the most extraordinary thing about the passage. The most extraordinary thing is what isn't said, but what provides the link between the two puzzles that we are otherwise facing, like the archaeologist trying to put together a fossil and a bone.

To begin with, we have an unanswered comment from Martha. Good old Martha, we think, always fussing and anxious, wanting to do her best, even at a time like this. 'Master,' she says, 'you can't take the stone away! There'll be a smell!' She knows perfectly well that a human body, particularly in a warm climate, will begin to putrefy within at most three days of death. That's why many in that part of the world bury their dead the very first day.

John doesn't have Jesus answer her, except with an oblique comment: if she believes, she will see God's glory. Somehow, what he is going to do will achieve that. But the question remains: what has happened to Lazarus's body? Will it have started to decay?

The other unexplained bit of evidence is what Jesus says when they take the stone away. He doesn't pray that he will now have the power to raise Lazarus. He thanks the father that he has heard him. And he adds an odd little extra sentence about wanting to show the people around that they should believe in him.

How do we put these two bits of evidence together and make sense of them?

John has omitted – but surely wants us to understand, and to be struck all the more powerfully for having to work it out – that when they took the stone away from the tomb *there was no smell*. From that moment on, Jesus knew that Lazarus was not dead, or was dead no longer. His body had not begun to decompose. All that was required now was a word of command, and he would come out, a shuffling, sightless figure, to be unwrapped and released into the world of life and light. But we are left pondering how Jesus had got to that point.

There is only one conclusion that we can draw, and it's very striking. In those two silent days the other side of the Jordan (11.6), before he even told the disciples of the problem, he was praying: praying that, though Lazarus would die, he would be preserved from corruption; praying that, when eventually they arrived at Bethany, the body in the tomb would be whole and complete, ready to be summoned back into life. And when they took the stone away he knew that his prayer had been answered.

This, of course, raises the other question which looms up behind this story. The disciples warned Jesus that to go back to Judaea again was to court death (11.8). Thomas, gloomily accepting this as inevitable, proposes that they go and die with him (11.16). Jesus, meanwhile, has been praying for a dear and now dead friend, praying that his body will not decay in the days after death and burial, but that he will be ready to come back to life. We cannot but connect the two, the fate of Lazarus and the fate of Jesus. We cannot but suppose that Jesus, in praying for Lazarus and then raising him to life, was aware that he was walking towards his own death, and praying his way into the father's will for what would happen thereafter.

Of course, there are differences. Lazarus came back into ordinary human life. For him, the process of death was simply reversed. He could still become ill again. One day, he too would die (and there were some who wanted to make that happen sooner rather than later, as 12.10 indicates). But the journey Jesus would make would be *through* death and out the other side into a new sort of life.

For the moment, we pause and reflect not only on the power of God but on the faith and prayer of Jesus. So often we find two or three parts of our life which pose us the same sort of puzzle that we find in this text, things that should go together, but we can't quite see how.

We should remember that in this story the unspoken clue to it all was prayer and faith. If Jesus needed to spend time praying and waiting, how much more will we.

For reflection or discussion

- Reflect on the dramatic scene of Lazarus being raised from the dead. What emotions does this event evoke in you? Consider how the mixture of horror and joy in this moment reflects the complexities of life and faith.
- Consider the role of prayer and faith in this passage. Reflect on Jesus' silent days of prayer before raising Lazarus and his awareness of his own impending death. How does prayer help you to navigate the puzzles and complexities you encounter?

Friday

Love one another: John 13.31–38

31Jesus began to speak.

'Now the son of man is glorified!' he said. 'Now God is glorified in him! 32And if God is glorified in him, God will glorify him in himself, and glorify him at once. 33Children, I'm only with you a little longer. You will look for me, and, as I said to the Judaeans that where I was going they couldn't come, so I'm saying the same to you now.

34'I'm giving you a new commandment, and it's this: love one another! Just as I have loved you, so you must love one another. 35This is how everybody will know that you are my disciples, if you have love for each other.'

36Simon Peter spoke up.

'Master,' he said, 'where are you going?'

'Where I'm going', replied Jesus, 'you can't follow me just now. You will follow later, though.'

³⁷'Master,' Peter replied, 'why can't I follow you now? I will lay down my life for you!'

³⁸'Will you really lay down your life for me?' smiled Jesus. 'I'm telling you the solemn truth: by the time the cock crows you will have disowned me three times.'

This is where the 'farewell discourses', as they are often called, really start. The disciples ask questions from time to time, but from now until the end of chapter 16 Jesus is explaining to them the fact that he is 'going away', and that they can't follow him just yet.

These chapters have often rightly been seen as among the most precious and intimate in the New Testament. They are full of comfort, challenge and hope, full of the deep and strange personal relationship that Jesus longs to have with each of his followers. We shouldn't be surprised that they are also full of some of the richest theological insights, of a sense of discovering who the true God is, and what he's doing in the world and in us. Where you find true devotion, you often find rich theology, and vice versa. Shallow thinking and shallow loving often keep company.

This is only the second time that Jesus has spoken of the son of man being 'glorified' (the other is 12.23). Before this moment he has spoken of *God* being glorified, and of the 'son of man' being 'lifted up'. Now he puts the two together. As in Daniel 7, 'one like a son of man' will be exalted, coming on the clouds to the Ancient of Days, and the whole scene will be the moment of God's glory, revealing who the true God is, over against the dark forces of the world that have resisted him and trampled upon his worshippers. You can feel the excitement in verses 31–32: glory, glory, glory, glory! Jesus is overwhelmed with glory, with the coming events as the unveiling of God's glory, with his own vocation rushing towards its conclusion and bringing God glory.

He is also overwhelmed by the fact that he is going to leave the disciples behind. He has only been with them a short while, and now he must go. Few teachers would be able to face such a moment without qualms. The disciples have learnt so little, understood so little, grasped so little of what their wonderful master has been doing in their midst. How will they cope without him?

The next three chapters will provide the answer, as Jesus makes the disciples solemn promises about the coming holy spirit who will continue to guide them as he himself has done. But before he even gets to that, he has something else to offer them: the simplest, clearest and hardest command of all. Love one another.

He describes it as a 'new commandment'. Love, of course, is central in many parts of the Old Testament. The book Leviticus (19.18) commanded the Israelites to love their neighbours as themselves. But the newness isn't so much a matter of never having heard words like this before. It's a matter of the mode of this love, the depth and type of this love: love one another *in the same way that I have loved you*.

This is to be the badge that the Christian community wears before the watching world. As we read verse 35 we are bound to cringe with shame at the way in which professing Christians have treated each other down the years. We have turned the gospel into a weapon of our own various cultures. We have hit each other over the head with it, burnt each other at the stake with it. We have defined the 'one another' so tightly that it means only 'love the people who reinforce your own sense of who you are'.

Like a child returning to the question he wanted to ask after the conversation has moved on elsewhere, Peter harks back to what Jesus said in verse 33, even though verses 34 and 35 contain some of the most beautiful and challenging words ever spoken. Once again he and Jesus banter to and fro, with Peter blustering away and saying whatever comes into his head. This time, though, the conversation suddenly runs into a brick wall. Peter doesn't realize what he's said. 'Where are you going? I'll follow you! I *want* to follow you! I'll lay down my life for you . . .'

'Will you really, Peter?' replies Jesus, and we can see the soft, sad smile as he says it. 'Is it really *you* who's going to lay down *your* life for *me*? Actually, Peter, I hate to say it, but what *you* are about to do is something rather different . . .'

We love Peter because he is so like the rest of us. And we love Jesus because he is so gentle with him, so loving, even within the sadness and the challenge and the glory that is to come.

For reflection or discussion

- What does it mean to love others in the same way that Jesus loved his disciples? Reflect on instances when Christians have failed to love one another and explore ways to foster a more authentic and inclusive love within the church today.

- How does Peter's eagerness and bluster reflect our own human tendencies? Consider times when your own commitments may have fallen short and on the gentle and loving nature of Jesus in response to your imperfections. How can you learn from this interaction and grow in faith and discipleship?

Saturday

Obeying and loving: John 15.9–17

[9]'As the father loved me,' Jesus continued, 'so I loved you. Remain in my love. [10]If you keep my commands, you will remain in my love, just as I have kept my father's commands, and remain in his love. [11]I've said these things to you so that my joy may be in you, and so that your joy may be full.

[12]'This is my command: love one another, in the same way that I loved you. [13]No one has a love greater than this, to lay down your life for your friends. [14]You are my friends, if you do what I tell you. [15]I'm not calling you "servants" any longer; servants don't know what their master is doing. But I've called

you "friends", because I've let you know everything I heard from my father.

¹⁶'You didn't choose me. I chose you, and I appointed you to go and bear fruit, fruit that will last. Then the father will give you whatever you ask in my name. ¹⁷This is my command to you: love one another.'

Like an innocent child wandering alone into a kitchen and pressing the switches that will set the house on fire, some biblical texts have been taken out of their original setting and used in ways that would have horrified the original speaker or writer. Here in this passage we have one with exactly that history.

'No one', said Jesus, 'has a love greater than this, to lay down your life for your friends' (verse 13). That is true, gloriously true. Indeed, Jesus was on his way to his own execution as the most dramatic example of the point (see 10.11; 13.1). The cross is clearly in view here, when Jesus says that laying down your life for your friends is the highest form of love, and then says, 'And you, of course, are my friends' (verse 14). But during the First World War (1914–18), this text was used again and again, in sermons and lectures, set to music and sung by great choirs, with one single meaning: therefore *you*, young man – they were mostly young men – must go off to the front line, do what you're told and if necessary die for your country.

They did, in their tens of thousands. God honours, I believe, the self-sacrifice and dedication of those who sincerely and devoutly feel they are doing their duty. But I also believe God judges those who use texts like this as a convenient rhetorical trick to put moral pressure on other people, when what they need is a bit of moral pressure on themselves to ask: Why are we doing this at all? If we must have a war, is this really the best way of fighting it? Are these 'sacrifices' (another convenient 'religious' word; people spoke of 'the final sacrifice', forgetting that in the Bible human sacrifice was condemned over and over again) the best way both of winning the war and of preparing ourselves for the world that will need rebuilding after it's all over?

The easy identification of 'our' side with God's side has been a major problem ever since Christianity became the official religion of the Roman state in the fourth century. Ironically, as Western Europe has become less and less Christian in terms of its practice, its leaders seem to have made this identification more and more, so that both sides in the major world wars of the twentieth century were staffed, as we have already noted, by Christian chaplains praying for victory.

This sits uneasily alongside a passage like this one, where the talk is of love, not war. In a world of danger and wickedness, it won't do for everyone to pretend there are no hard decisions to be made. But precisely one of the great dangers, and great wickednesses, of the world is the very common belief that fighting is a fine thing, that war is a useful way of settling disputes, and that, to put it crudely, might is right. One of the reasons human civilization has struggled to promote justice is the recognition that things aren't that easy. And justice, at its best, knows that it has only a negative function: to clear the decks and leave the world open for people to love one another.

You can't legislate for love; but God, through Jesus, can command you to love. Discovering the difference between what law cannot achieve and what God can and does achieve is one of the great arts of being human, and of being Christian. In the present passage we are brought in on the secret of it all.

The 'command' to love is given by one who has himself done everything that love can do. When a mother loves a child, she creates the context in which the child is free to love her in return. When a ruler really does love his or her subjects, and when this becomes clear by generous and warm-hearted actions, he or she creates a context in which the subjects can and will love them in return. The parody of this, seen with awesome clarity in George Orwell's book *Nineteen Eighty-Four*, is when the totalitarian ruler ('Big Brother'), who has done nothing but oppress and terrify his subjects, nevertheless orders them to love him. And the devastating climax, after the initially resisting subjects have been brainwashed, is that it works. At the end of the book, the hero is, in a sense, happy. 'He loved Big Brother.' And the reader knows that at this moment the hero has ceased to be truly human.

Jesus, though, issues the command that we are to love one another, and so to remain in his love, because he has acted out, and will act out, the greatest thing that love can do. He has come to make us more human, not less. He has come to give us freedom and joy (verse 11), not slavery and a semi-human stupor. He has come so that we can bear fruit that will last (verse 16), whether in terms of a single life changed because we loved somebody as Jesus loved us, or in terms of a single decision that we had to take, a single task we had to perform, through which, though we couldn't see it at the time, the world became a different place. Love makes both the lover and the beloved more truly human.

At the heart of it all is the humility that comes from knowing who's in charge. 'You didn't choose me; I chose you' (verse 16). I was once asked, on the radio, which religion I would choose if I could. I pointed out that the idea of 'choosing your religion' was a mistake in the first place. Religions are not items on the supermarket shelf that we can pick and choose – though many today try to run their lives that way. Or, if they are, you'd have to say that following Jesus wasn't a 'religion'. It is a personal relationship of love and loyalty to the one who has loved us more than we can begin to imagine. And the test of that love and loyalty remains the simple, profound, dangerous and difficult command: love one another.

For reflection or discussion

- How can Christians reconcile Jesus' teaching on love with the realities of a world filled with danger and wickedness? Think about approaches to conflict resolution and the pursuit of justice that prioritize love and compassion over violence.

- Consider the idea of choosing a religion versus embracing a personal relationship with Jesus based on love and loyalty. How does this understanding challenge the consumeristic approach to religion prevalent today?

Week 4
Jesus among enemies

Monday

Loving your enemies: Luke 6.27–36

[27]'This is my word', Jesus continued, 'for those of you who are listening: love your enemies! Do good to people who hate you! [28]Bless people who curse you! Pray for people who treat you badly!

[29]'If someone hits you on the cheek – offer him the other one! If someone takes away your coat – don't stop him taking your shirt! [30]Give to everyone who asks you, and don't ask for things back when people have taken them.

[31]'Whatever you want people to do to you, do that to them. [32]If you love those who love you, what credit is that to you? Think about it: even sinners love people who love them. [33]Or again, if you do good only to people who do good to you, what credit is that to you? Sinners do that too. [34]If you lend only to people you expect to get things back from, what credit is that to you? Even sinners lend to sinners to get paid back. [35]No: love your enemies, do good and lend without expecting any return. Your reward will be great! You will be children of the Highest! He is generous, you see, to the stingy and wicked. [36]You must be merciful, just as your father is merciful.'

One of the greatest Jewish scholars to write about Jesus in the modern age was David Flusser, who taught for many years at the Hebrew

University in Jerusalem. But not everyone approved of his scholarship; and one of his most brilliant students, visiting a university elsewhere, was once given a very low mark by the professor simply because of being associated with Flusser himself. Then, some time later, a student of that other professor came to study with Flusser. His work was not very good, but Flusser insisted on grading it with an 'A'. His teaching assistant protested: how could he do that, particularly after what the other professor had done? 'Give him an A,' insisted Flusser. 'This I have learned from Jesus.'

The kingdom that Jesus preached and lived was all about a glorious, uproarious, absurd generosity. Think of the best thing you can do for the worst person, and go ahead and do it. Think of what you'd really like someone to do for you, and do it for them. Think of the people to whom you are tempted to be nasty, and lavish generosity on them instead. These instructions have a fresh, spring-like quality. They are all about new life bursting out energetically, like flowers growing through concrete and startling everyone with their colour and vigour.

But are they achievable? Well, yes and no. Jesus' point was not to provide his followers with a new rule book, a list of dos and don'ts that you could tick off one by one, and sit back satisfied at the end of a successful moral day. The point was to inculcate, and illustrate, an attitude of heart, a lightness of spirit in the face of all that the world can throw at you. And at the centre of it is the thing that motivates and gives colour to the whole: you are to be like this *because that's what God is like*. God is generous to all people, generous (in the eyes of the stingy) to a fault: he provides good things for all to enjoy, the undeserving as well as the deserving. He is astonishingly merciful (anyone who knows their own heart truly, and still goes on experiencing God's grace and love, will agree with this); how can we, his forgiven children, be any less? Only when people discover that this is the sort of God they are dealing with will they have any chance of making this way of life their own.

In fact, this list of instructions is all about which God you believe in – and about the way of life that follows as a result. We must admit with shame that large sections of Christianity down the years seem to have known little or nothing of the God Jesus was talking about. Much that has called itself by the name of Jesus seems to have believed instead in a gloomy God, a penny-pinching God, a God whose only concern is to make life difficult, and salvation nearly impossible. But, by the same token, this passage gives the lie to the old idea (which was around in Jesus' day as well as our own) that all religions are really the same, that all gods are really variations on the same theme. This God is different. If you lived in a society where everyone believed in this God, there wouldn't be any violence. There wouldn't be any revenge. There wouldn't be any divisions of class or caste. Property and possessions wouldn't be nearly as important as making sure your neighbour was all right. Imagine if even a few people around you took Jesus seriously and lived like that. Life would be exuberant, different, astonishing. People would stare.

And of course people did stare when Jesus did it himself. The reason why crowds gathered was that power was flowing out of Jesus, and people were being healed. His whole life was one of exuberant generosity, giving all he'd got to give to everyone who needed it. He was speaking of what he knew: the extravagant love of his father, and the call to live a lavish human life in response. And finally, when they struck him on the cheek and ripped the coat and shirt off his back, he went on loving and forgiving. He didn't show love only to his friends, but to his enemies, weeping over the city that had rejected his plea for peace. He was the true embodiment of the God of whom he spoke.

For reflection or discussion

- Reflect on the contrast between Jesus' perception of God and the perceptions held by some sections of Christianity throughout history. How can you cultivate an attitude of heart and a lightness of spirit that reflect the generosity and mercy of God?

- In what practical ways can you demonstrate love, forgiveness and generosity to others, even when it seems difficult or goes against social norms?

Tuesday

Teachings on the sabbath: Mark 2.23–28

[23]One sabbath, Jesus was walking through the cornfields. His disciples made their way along, plucking corn as they went.

[24]'Look here,' said the Pharisees to him, 'why are they doing something illegal on the sabbath?'

[25]'Haven't you ever read what David did,' replied Jesus, 'when he was in difficulties, and he and his men got hungry? [26]He went into God's house (this was when Abiathar was high priest), and ate the "bread of the presence", which only the priests were allowed to eat – and he gave it to the people with him.

[27]'The sabbath was made for humans,' he said, 'not humans for the sabbath; [28]so the son of man is master even of the sabbath.'

The twentieth century saw a great deal of secret police activity. The KGB in the Soviet Union, and the Stasi in East Germany, were legends in their own lifetime during the Communist period. Several countries in Central and South America, and some parts of Asia, have thriving secret police forces that are rightly feared by ordinary folk.

That's the picture we naturally think of when we find Pharisees spying on Jesus and his followers; and it's actually very misleading. The Pharisees were *not* in any sense an official secret police force, in Jesus' day or at any other time. They were an unofficial party that had been active as a religious and political pressure group for nearly 200 years by Jesus' time. (Most political parties in modern Western democracies are much younger than that, at least in their present form.) The Pharisees were entirely self-chosen, and had no authority to make laws or enforce them. They did, though, have considerable influence on ordinary people, who respected their expertise in Israel's ancestral laws and traditions.

If they weren't like a secret police, then what were they like? Some were wise, devout, holy men. Some, though, behaved like nosey journalists in the modern world, setting themselves up as the self-appointed guardians of public morality and spying on people in the public eye. That's what seems to be going on here. They probably wouldn't have bothered to check on an ordinary group of people walking through cornfields on the sabbath. But Jesus and his followers weren't ordinary people. They were already marked out because of what Jesus was doing and the implicit claims he was making. They needed watching, to see if they were loyal Jews or not. Just as anyone who even looks as though they might run for office in some modern democracies will find the journalists taking a sudden interest in their everyday private behaviour, to see if there's any mud that might stick, so Jesus' growing reputation attracted similar attention.

Keeping the sabbath was, of course, one of the Ten Commandments, and it had been reinforced by the prophets and by subsequent Jewish teaching. It was one of the things that marked out the Jews, over the centuries, from their pagan neighbours – one of the things that reminded them that they were God's people. It wasn't an odd moral commandment which people observed to earn merit or favour with God; it was a sign that they belonged to the true God, the creator of the world, who had himself rested on the seventh day. Just as today, in some parts of Jerusalem, the successors of the Pharisees watch carefully to see that everybody in the area is observing the sabbath properly, so in Jesus' day some Pharisees checked up at least on would-be leaders and new movements.

Jesus' reply is a bit of a tease, but packs a strong punch. He doesn't deny that the disciples are out of line with traditional sabbath observance, but he pleads special circumstances and scriptural precedent.

He puts himself on a par with King David in the period when David, already anointed by Samuel but not yet enthroned (because Saul was still king), was on the run, gathering support, waiting for his time to come. That's a pretty heavy claim: the implication is that Jesus is the true king, marked out by God (presumably in his baptism) but not yet recognized and enthroned. He therefore has the right, when he and his people are hungry, to by-pass the normal regulations. In other words, this kind of sabbath-breaking, far from being an act of casual or wanton civil disobedience, is a deliberate sign, like the refusal to fast: a sign that the king is here, that the kingdom is breaking in, that instead of waiting for the old creation to come to its point of rest the new creation is already bursting upon the old world.

All of this is summed up in the riddle at the end, which probably puzzled Jesus' hearers as much as it does people today. It is a combined comment about the sabbath and about Jesus' own authority. This is the second time we meet 'the son of man' in Mark; the setting seems to reinforce one particular meaning the phrase could have, namely the messianic figure which first-century Jews discovered in Daniel 7, whose arrival and enthronement signals the start of God's kingdom. Jesus doesn't mean that just any human being is 'Lord of the sabbath', but that the Messiah, the true representative human being, has authority over institutions that might otherwise repress human beings.

Jesus' action, and its explanation, was a coded messianic claim, a claim that in him the new day was dawning in which even Israel's God-given laws would be seen in a new light. How much more are the institutions and local customs of ordinary societies to be judged by the humanizing rule of the son of man!

For reflection or discussion

- Explore the character and role of the Pharisees in Jesus' time. How did they exert influence and monitor the actions of others? What parallels can be drawn between their actions and contemporary instances of moral policing or scrutiny of public figures?

- Why did the Pharisees confront Jesus in this way? What does Jesus' response reveal about his understanding of his own identity and authority?

Wednesday

The healing of a man with a withered hand: Mark 3.1–6

¹Jesus went to the synagogue. There was a man there with a withered hand. ²People were watching to see if Jesus would heal him on the sabbath, so that they could frame a charge against him.

³'Stand up', said Jesus to the man with the withered hand, 'and come out here.' And he said to them, ⁴'Is it lawful to do good on the sabbath, or to do evil? To save life or to kill?' They stayed quiet.

⁵He was deeply upset at their hard-heartedness, and looked round at them angrily. Then he said to the man, 'Stretch out your hand.' He stretched it out – and his hand was restored. ⁶The Pharisees went out right away and began to plot with the Herodians against Jesus, trying to find a way to destroy him.

It's difficult for me to remember what life was like when I was a boy. It's even harder for young people today to imagine what it was like in their own country fifty years ago. Almost everywhere has changed drastically. In England, one change is particularly noticeable. When I was young, everybody kept Sunday as a very special day. Just a few decades ago, in the average English town, there were no shops open on Sundays; there was no professional sport – yes, no football, no racing; everything was very, very quiet. Nothing like today.

A cartoon of the time sums up the attitude, and the problem. An anxious father, worried about what the neighbours may say, tells his little girl she mustn't play with her hoop in the street on Sunday. She should go into the back garden. 'Isn't it Sunday in the back garden?' asks the girl.

The irony, of course, is that whenever Jesus is faced with the question of sabbath observance he moves in the opposite direction. He appears to take a shockingly liberal line. This has been a problem for strict Sunday-observance enthusiasts, who for centuries have cheerfully transferred the Jewish commandment of observing the seventh day of the week and switched it to observing the first day – something the New Testament never actually does (though it's clear the early Christians met for worship on the first day, the day they celebrated Jesus' resurrection). Today most Western Christians, frankly, are in a bit of a muddle on the issue. We all know that the old-style sabbath observance as a social phenomenon has gone for good. Even though we mostly believe that one day off from work in a week is a healthy ideal, it's not at all obvious how best, or most appropriately, to achieve it.

These thoughts and puzzles may crowd into our minds when we read about Jesus healing on the sabbath; but if we're going to see what it meant at the time we have to go back, not just to the 'sabbath' observance of our (or at least my) childhood, but to the world of first-century Palestine. For a Jew in Jesus' world, the sabbath had all that mixture of social pressure and legal sanction, but it meant much more as well. It was a badge of Jewishness for people who'd been persecuted and killed simply for being Jewish. It was a national flag that spoke of freedom to come, of hope for the great Day of Rest when God would finally liberate Israel from pagan oppression. It looked back to the creation of the world, and to the Exodus from Egypt, and it marked out those who kept it as God's special people, God's faithful people, God's hoping people. It was, after all, a commandment deeply embedded in the Jewish scriptures.

So why does Jesus appear to drive a coach and horses through it? Because it had become a weapon. It had become a sign of his fellow

Jews' commitment to a fierce and exclusive nationalism. Along with other badges and flags, it spoke now not of Israel as the light of the world but of Israel as the children of light and the rest of the world as remaining in darkness. And this attitude, as so easily happens when religion and nationalism are wedded tightly together, spilled over into popular attitudes even towards fellow-Jews. For many groups, it wasn't enough to be a loyal Jew; one had to be a better loyal Jew than the other lot. And in this no-win situation the whole point of the commandment – celebrating God's creation and redemption, past, present and future – had been lost sight of. The rule mattered more than the reality.

Jesus' verdict on that was that it constituted 'hard-heartedness' – one of the regular charges that the prophets levelled against law-*breaking* Israelites in days gone by. Like the wilderness generation under Moses, his contemporaries were unable to see and celebrate what God was actually doing in front of their noses. So he puts the question in its starkest terms, in words dripping with irony: is it legal to do good on the sabbath, or only to do evil? Is it legal to make people alive, or only to kill them? If the sabbath speaks of creation and redemption, the answer is obvious – and if the current interpretation of the rules says otherwise, so much the worse for the current interpretation of the rules.

Of course, it's not clear that what Jesus actually did – speaking a word of command, and leaving the man to stretch out his own hand, hardly a breach of sabbath observance – was breaking the official or even the unofficial interpretation of the sabbath. But his approach and attitude were clearly on a collision course with those of the self-appointed guardians of the ancestral traditions. In a move that anticipates again the whole larger story Mark is telling, the unofficial leaders of Jewish opinion (the Pharisees) get together with their natural enemies (the supporters of Herod Antipas, whom the Pharisees normally regarded as a dangerous traitor to Judaism). Why did they do that?

The Pharisees had no power themselves. If they were going to attack Jesus, they needed to make unlikely alliances. Thus it would be at the end, when Caiaphas and Pilate together sent Jesus to his death; thus it would be not long afterwards, when the young Pharisee Saul of Tarsus obtained authority from the chief priests to persecute the church. Thus it was in this instance, with local Galilean Pharisees making common cause with the supporters of Herod Antipas, in a futile attempt to do away with Jesus.

For reflection or discussion

- Explore the relationship between religion and nationalism, as exemplified by sabbath observance during Jesus' time. How can the merging of religious and nationalistic identities lead to exclusivity and the marginalization of others? Can you think of instances where religious rules have been 'weaponized' and made to do a job for which they were never intended?

- Keeping the sabbath was one of the Ten Commandments. Can we recapture the true spirit of the sabbath in a world where economic forces are frequently far more dehumanizing than the abused sabbath law ever was? How can we learn again what it means to live in a rhythm of work and rest, and to help one another in our wider society to do the same, without becoming legalists in the process?

Thursday

Adultery and hypocrisy: John 8.1–11

[1]Jesus went to the Mount of Olives. [2]In the morning he went back to the Temple. All the people came to him, and he sat down and taught them.

[3]The scribes and Pharisees brought a woman who had been caught out in adultery. They stood her out in the middle.

⁴'Teacher,' they said to him. 'This woman was caught in the very act of adultery. ⁵In the law, Moses commanded us to stone people like this. What do you say?'

⁶They said this to test him, so that they could frame a charge against him.

Jesus squatted down and wrote with his finger on the ground. ⁷When they went on pressing the question, he got up and said to them, 'Whichever of you is without sin should throw the first stone at her.'

⁸And once again he squatted down and wrote on the ground.

⁹When they heard that, they went off one by one, beginning with the oldest. Jesus was left alone, with the woman still standing there.

¹⁰Jesus looked up.

'Where are they, woman?' he asked. 'Hasn't anybody condemned you?'

¹¹'Nobody, sir,' she replied.

'Well, then,' said Jesus, 'I don't condemn you either! Off you go – and from now on don't sin again!'

Two women were brought before the young king. They were prostitutes, and shared a house. Both had given birth, but the son of one of them had died. Now both were claiming the living son as their own. How could anyone tell (in the days before DNA testing!) which one was speaking the truth?

The king gave his judgment. Bring a sword, he said, and cut the boy in two. Each woman can have half of him.

The instant reaction of the two women told him the truth. One of them agreed with the verdict. The other one begged that the boy should live, even if her rival was allowed to keep him. No question which was the true mother.

The king was, of course, Solomon; the story is told in 1 Kings 3.16–28. It was the kind of thing that got him his reputation for possessing remarkable wisdom. And this is the kind of story that people in the first century would think of when they heard this story about Jesus, the woman taken in adultery, and the men taken in . . . hypocrisy.

In the previous chapter, John 7, Jesus had been teaching in the Temple during the festival of Tabernacles, and the crowds and authorities were getting increasingly interested in asking who he was and what he was about. John 8 has an altogether darker tone, with Jesus accusing the Judaeans of wilfully misunderstanding him, failing to grasp what he's saying, and wanting to kill him, because they are following the dictates of 'their father, the devil'. Chapter 8 contains some of the harshest things Jesus is ever recorded as saying. What has happened?

It is as though Jesus has come face to face with the real problem at the heart of the Judaean attitude – to him, to God, to themselves, to their national vocation. Something has caught Jesus' attention, and has made him realize just how steeped in their own patterns of thinking his Judaean contemporaries have become – and how devastatingly unlike God's patterns of thinking they are.

The chapter begins with people wanting to stone a woman to death; it ends with them wanting to stone Jesus. Perhaps that, too, is trying to tell us something.

The story is a classic example of Jesus' own wisdom, the sort of wisdom that kings were expected to display. (Remember that the underlying question of this whole part of John's gospel is whether or not Jesus is the Messiah, the true king.) The story turns on the trap that the scribes and Pharisees had set for Jesus. They suspected that he would want to tell the woman that her sins had been forgiven; but that would mean he was teaching people to ignore something in the law of Moses.

Already we can sense the temperature of the situation rising, and with it Jesus' anger. They are using the woman, however guilty she might be of serious sin, simply as a tool in their attack on him. And, in so doing, they are enjoying their sense of moral superiority over her, as well as their sense of having put Jesus in a corner he can't easily escape from.

Nobody knows, of course, what Jesus was writing on the ground. (In the ancient world, teachers often used to write or draw in the dust; that's how some of the great geometry teachers would explain things, in the days before PCs and iPads.) We can guess if we like; maybe he was writing lists of other sins, including hypocrisy. Maybe he was making a point about sins of the eye and heart, as in Matthew 5.28. Or maybe he was just doodling, treating their question with the contempt it deserved.

But his answer when it comes, though apparently risky (supposing one of them had had the arrogance to go ahead?), is devastating. When you point the finger at someone else, there are three fingers pointing back at you. He hasn't said the law of Moses was wrong; only that, if we're going to get serious about it, we should all find ourselves guilty. And one by one they get the point and go away.

The story certainly doesn't mean – as some people have tried to make it mean – that adultery doesn't matter. That's not the point at all. Jesus' last words to the woman are extremely important. If she has been forgiven – if she's been rescued from imminent death – she must live by that forgiveness. *Forgiveness is not the same thing as 'tolerance'.* Being forgiven doesn't mean that sin doesn't matter. On the contrary: 'forgiveness' means that sin *does* matter – but that God is choosing to set it aside.

And the sin that matters even more, as the rest of the chapter makes clear, is the deep-rooted sin which uses the God-given law as a means of making oneself out to be righteous, when in fact it is meant to shine the light of God's judgment into the dark places of the heart. By confronting this sin, Jesus has put himself in the firing line from which he has just rescued the woman. If you read chapter 8 as it stands from beginning to end you may start to see a pattern which will continue through to Jesus' death. This is part of what it means, John seems to be saying, that Jesus is God's lamb, the one who takes away the sin of the world.

For reflection or discussion

- How does Jesus' response to the scribes and Pharisees in this passage challenge their self-righteousness and expose their hypocrisy? Consider the dangers of using moral superiority as a tool to attack others and the importance of self-reflection in your own judgments.

- Explore the theme of sin and self-righteousness in the larger context of the chapter. How does Jesus' confrontation with the scribes and Pharisees shed light on the deeper issues of the human heart?

Friday

On paying taxes to Caesar: Mark 12.13–17

[13]They sent some Pharisees to Jesus, and some Herodians, to try to trick him into saying the wrong thing.

[14]'Teacher,' they said, 'we know you are a man of integrity; you don't regard anybody as special. You don't bother about the outward show people put up; you teach God's way truly.

'Well then: is it lawful to give tribute to Caesar or not? Should we pay it, or shouldn't we?'

[15]He knew the game they were playing. 'Why are you trying to trap me?' he said. 'Bring me a tribute-coin; let me look at it.'

[16]They brought one to him.

'This image,' he asked, 'whose is it? And whose is this superscription?'

'Caesar's,' they replied.

[17]'Well then,' said Jesus, 'give Caesar back what belongs to Caesar – and give God back what belongs to God!'

They were astonished at him.

I have on my desk one of the tribute-pennies from the reign of Tiberius Caesar. It is almost certainly the type that features in this story. It's about the size of my thumbnail, but you can make out the writing quite clearly – and the imperial head of Tiberius. You don't have to look at it for too long to see that this conversation wasn't simply about taxation policy.

That was itself bad enough, though. Paying taxes to Rome was a running sore to devout Jews. It wasn't only the cost, though for many that would be serious (they would also pay local taxes, Temple taxes and, for those in Galilee, taxes to Herod as well). It was what the tax represented. The Jews celebrated the fact that they were God's free people, but they agonized over the reality that it wasn't true. Ever since the Babylonian invasion half a millennium before, they had been ruled by others. Under the Hasmoneans, in the period roughly 163 BC to 63 BC, they were semi-independent; but since then Rome had taken over. And where Rome ruled, Rome taxed, and Rome was hated for it.

But the coin itself went further. Jews were forbidden to make carved images. They debated whether this included images of plants and flowers, but images of human beings were out of the question; and here is Tiberius, staring coldly out at the world from every small Roman coin. And the writing! Around the head the words say, in Latin: 'Augustus Tiberius, son of the divine Augustus'. On the other side, it says: 'High Priest' (the emperors were routinely high priests of the main Roman cult). 'Son of a god'; 'high priest' – if the Romans had gone out of their way to be offensive to the Jews, they could hardly have done it better. And when Jesus, the true king, the son of God, is standing there in the Temple ruled by the Jewish chief priest, the irony could hardly be sharper.

So it was (what we would call) a religious question, not simply a political or social one, that faced Jesus. Some devout Jews were so shocked by this type of coin that they would try never to touch or use one (they could use Jewish coins instead), or even perhaps to look at one. Jesus, by asking his questioners to produce a coin, isn't exactly saying that he wouldn't normally touch the stuff himself, but he is at least embarrassing them by making them find one for him to look at.

Here, again, the Pharisees and Herodians are acting together. Their trap is clear. They are trying to force Jesus either to support the paying of taxes to Rome, thus alienating the crowds, or to denounce the tax, in which case they could tell the governor, Pontius Pilate, that Jesus was guilty of a straightforward capital charge, namely inciting revolt. But they reckoned without Jesus' brilliant response.

To understand what he meant, a word about the background. Two hundred years earlier, one of the slogans of the Maccabean revolt against the Syrians had been 'pay back the Gentiles what they deserve – and obey the commands of the law!' (1 Maccabees 2.68). This put into a crisp double command the Jewish duty to the Gentiles and to God. What the first half meant was: give as good as you get. In other words, vengeance: repayment in kind for the violence the Gentiles had used.

Now a very different revolt is under way. Jesus had opposed violent revolution, and his kingdom-movement was attacking a deeper and more far-reaching evil than simply pagan domination. He is not going to be drawn into the sterile should-we/shouldn't-we debate. Nor is he giving a timeless ethical ruling which settles once for all the relationship between church and state – though some have mistakenly tried to build such a theory on this very narrow foundation. He is hitting the ball back over the net at twice the speed it came. We need to separate out three different things he's doing, each of which takes them completely by surprise.

First, 'give Caesar what belongs to Caesar' can be taken, of course, as a way of saying 'yes, pay the tax', but without the sting of 'yes, submit to the Romans as your masters'. The fact that Jesus has drawn attention to the blasphemous image and writing gives his command the flavour of 'send this filthy stuff back where it came from!' It is contemptuous, without opening Jesus to the charge of sedition.

Second, though, it nicely echoes the Maccabean slogan. 'Give the pagans what they deserve'; or, if you like, 'pay the Gentiles back in their own coin'. It could be taken as a coded revolutionary slogan; after all, the kingdom of God is all about the one true God becoming king of the world, demoting the petty princelings who style themselves sons of God, high priests, or whatever. Yet again, in context, it doesn't leave Jesus open to a direct charge. His words are, after all, literally saying, 'yes, pay the tax'.

Third, the command to give God what belongs to God opens all kinds of further questions. Did he also mean that, because humans bear God's image, all humans owe themselves, their very lives, to God, and should give those lives back, as one might give a coin back to Caesar? Did he mean, standing there in the Temple courtyards, that the sacrificial system, which was supposed to be the way of giving God his due, needed to be superseded by a more complete worship? Did he mean – against the normal revolutionaries – that if you really gave your whole self to God you would discover that using violence to fight violence, using evil to fight evil, simply wouldn't do? I think he probably meant to hint at all of that, and perhaps even more.

What he didn't mean – despite many attempts to squash his words into this shape – was that you could divide human life, and the world, into two segments (the 'religious' part and the 'political' or 'social' part). That's a much later idea, which gained ground only in the eighteenth century. It has had a huge influence on the modern world, but is increasingly being seen today as at best inadequate and at worst dangerous. It would prevent, for instance, any Christian critique of public policy, including economic policy, which is sometimes sorely needed in our world. Jewish thought, and Christian thought as it emerged within Judaism, has always seen the entire world and everything in it as created by the one God. All aspects of it fall under his sovereign and saving rule.

To repeat, then: this passage wasn't designed as a full-scale statement of Christian truth on 'religion and society' or 'church and state'. It was a quick and sharp-edged quip for a particular occasion. But what Jesus said will bear a lot of thinking through and working out.

The kingdom of God goes beyond the sterile either/or questions which crafty people (often with flattery, as here) like to pose. God grant us wisdom to see to the heart of things, and to give ourselves wholly to our true God and king.

For reflection or discussion

- Examine Jesus' response to the question of paying taxes. How does his answer simultaneously challenge the oppressive Roman regime and expose the religious hypocrisy of his questioners? Discuss the complexities of Jesus' response and its implications for navigating the relationship between faith and politics today.
- Consider the distinction between the later concept of dividing life into 'religious' and 'secular' domains and the holistic view presented in Jewish and Christian thought. How does this help you understand your responsibility to engage with social, political and economic matters in light of your commitment to God's kingdom?

Saturday

The parable of the tenants: Matthew 21.33–46

[33]'Listen to another parable,' Jesus went on. 'Once upon a time there was a householder who planted a vineyard, built a wall for it, dug out a wine-press in it, and built a tower. Then he let it out to tenant farmers and went away on a journey.

[34]'When harvest time arrived, he sent his slaves to the farmers to collect his produce. [35]The farmers seized his slaves; they beat one, killed another, and stoned another. [36]Again he sent other slaves, more than before, and they treated them in the same way. [37]Finally he sent his son to them.

'"They'll respect my son," he said.

[38]'But the farmers saw the son.

'"This fellow's the heir!" they said among themselves. "Come on, let's kill him, and then we can take over the property!"

39'So they seized him, threw him out of the vineyard, and killed him.

40'Now then: when the vineyard owner returns, what will he do to those farmers?'

41'He'll kill them brutally, the wretches!' they said. 'And he'll lease the vineyard to other farmers who'll give him the produce at the right time.'

42'Did you never read what the Bible says?' said Jesus to them:
The stone the builders threw away
is now atop the corner;
it's from the Lord, all this, they say
and we looked on in wonder.

43'So then let me tell you this: God's kingdom is going to be taken away from you and given to a nation that will produce the goods. 44Anyone who falls on this stone will be smashed to pieces, and anyone it falls on will be crushed.'

45When the chief priests and the Pharisees heard his parables, they knew he was talking about them. 46They tried to arrest him, but they were afraid of the crowds, who regarded him as a prophet.

I had a dream last night, and the frustrating thing is that I can't remember what it was about. I know that when I woke up it seemed very important; indeed, so important that I wanted to write it down, but I didn't have the time. By the time I was fully awake it had gone, and I can't recall it. And yet I have known all day that it was significant, and that, if only I could get in touch with it, it might tell me something I need to know about myself or about the world.

Once upon a time there was an ancient king who posed a similar problem to his counsellors. He wanted to know what his dream meant, but he wouldn't tell them what it was. They, not being trained in modern psychology, objected strongly. Nobody has ever asked such a thing, they said. Whoever heard of such a request? If the king will only tell us his dream, then of course we will explain what it means. But the king refused – whether because he couldn't remember it, or because he was testing them, isn't quite clear. All seemed hopeless; until one wise man, getting his friends to pray for him, was granted special knowledge.

This was the king's dream. (The story is told in Daniel, chapter 2, one of many spectacular stories in that remarkable book.) He saw a huge statue: its head was made of gold, its chest and arms of silver, its middle and thighs of bronze, its legs of iron, and its feet of a mixture of iron and clay. Then there came a stone which struck the statue on its feet of iron and clay and smashed them; and the whole statue came crashing down and was broken into a million pieces. But the stone itself became a great mountain and filled the whole earth.

Once you knew a bit about dreams, and about ancient theories as to what they meant – especially if it was a king dreaming them – it wasn't too difficult to give an interpretation. And Daniel's interpretation of the king's dream lived on in the memory of the Jews from that day to the time of Jesus and beyond. It was all about the kingdoms of the world and the kingdom of God.

The kingdoms of the world were the successive kingdoms of gold, silver, bronze and iron. (The king who was having the dream, conveniently enough, ruled over the golden age.) Each would be less glorious than the one before; people in those days didn't usually believe that the world was getting better, but that it was getting worse. Finally there would be a brittle kingdom, like iron mixed with clay. Then there would come something different altogether.

A Stone – we'd better give it a capital letter for reasons that will soon appear – would smash the feet; in other words, it would destroy the last kingdom. The whole tottering structure of the empires of the world would come down with a crash. The Stone itself would grow to become a mountain: a new sort of kingdom, ruling the whole world in a new sort of way.

No Jew of Jesus' day would have had any difficulty figuring out what it all meant for them. The kingdoms of the world, starting with Babylon and Persia, had gone on until at last it was Rome's turn. And now, surely, was the moment for the Stone to appear! The Stone, they thought, meant God's Messiah, who would set up the kingdom of God by destroying the world's kingdoms and starting something quite new.

What has all this to do with the parable of the wicked farmers killing the owner's son? Just this: Jesus, interpreting his own story, quotes from two biblical passages, Psalm 118 and Daniel 2. The stone which the builders rejected has become the top cornerstone; it wouldn't fit anywhere else in the building, but it will go in the place of greatest honour. And the stone will crush anything that collides with it. He is the Stone, the Messiah, God's anointed; he has come to bring into being the kingdom of God through which the kingdoms of the world will shiver, shake and fall to the ground.

And why is that an interpretation of the parable? Because the Stone and the Son are the same. The Son the farmers rejected is vindicated when the owner comes and destroys them, and gives the vineyard to someone else. The Stone the builders rejected is vindicated when it goes in place at the top of the corner. And – just as in English the letters of the word 'son' are the same as the letters of the word 'stone', with two more added, so in Hebrew, by coincidence, the letters of the word *ben* (son) are the same as those of the word *eben* (stone), with one more added.

The whole story is therefore Jesus' way of explaining what was going on then and there. It is Jesus' perspective on the very events he was involved in – rejected by those he had come to, but destined to be vindicated by God. The vineyard owner is of course God; the vineyard is Israel; the farmers are Israel's officials, and the slaves are the earlier prophets, ending with John the Baptist. The son can only be Jesus himself.

106

It is a story full of depth, sorrow and power. It tells how he has now come to Jerusalem to confront the tenant farmers with God's demand for repentance, for Israel to be at last what it was called to be, the light of God's world. And it is the story of how Israel, through its official representatives, is going to refuse the demand, and will end up by killing him.

Why then the Stone? Because the last kingdom, the kingdom of iron mixed with clay, is perhaps not Rome after all. Maybe, from Jesus' point of view, it is the uneasy alliance of Herod and the chief priests. Maybe it is their shaky kingdom that will come crashing down when the Stone eventually falls on them. But before it can become the chief stone in the building it must first be rejected. And that, now, will not be long in coming.

For reflection or discussion

- What is the connection between the symbol of the Stone in the king's dream and the parable of the wicked farmers? Explore the significance of the Stone as a representation of God's kingdom and its impact on worldly powers.
- Consider the symbolism of the vineyard, the farmers, the son and the vineyard owner. How does this story shed light on Jesus' identity as the Messiah?

Week 5
Jesus in the city

Monday

Jesus grieves over Jerusalem: Luke 13.31–35

[31]Some Pharisees came up and spoke to Jesus.

'Get away from here,' they said, 'because Herod wants to kill you.'

[32]'Go and tell that fox,' replied Jesus, '"Look here: I'm casting out demons today and tomorrow, and completing my healings. I'll be finished by the third day. [33]But I have to continue my travels today, tomorrow and the day after that! It couldn't happen that a prophet would perish away from Jerusalem."

[34]'Jerusalem, Jerusalem! You kill the prophets, and stone the people sent to you! How many times did I want to collect your children, like a hen gathers her brood under her wings, and you would have none of it! [35]Look, your house has been abandoned. Let me tell you this: you will never see me until you are prepared to say, "Welcome with a blessing in the name of the Lord!"'

The house I live in was built after the Second World War. It replaced the much older one that stood here before, which was burnt to ashes one night in 1941, after a fire-bomb, dropped by an enemy aircraft, landed right on it. The people who lived in the house were helping to save another building nearby, and by the time they got water-pumps to this house, and the one next door, it was too late.

In the ancient world fire was an ever-present danger. It was of course necessary for many aspects of life, but without modern precautions and fire-fighting equipment it could easily get out of control. Roman writers of the New Testament period speak graphically about fires in Rome's crowded streets and tenements; the summer of AD 64 saw a fire in Rome that lasted a week and destroyed half the city. Though the word 'fire' does not occur in this passage, the powerful image Jesus uses here has it in mind. It isn't, however, in a city, but in a farmyard.

Fire is as terrifying to trapped animals as it is to people, if not more so. When a farmyard catches fire, the animals try to escape; but, if they cannot, some species have developed ways of protecting their young. The picture here is of a hen, gathering her chicks under her wings to protect them. There are stories of exactly this: after a farmyard fire, those cleaning up have found a dead hen, scorched and blackened – with live chicks sheltering under her wings. She has quite literally given her life to save them. It is a vivid and violent image of what Jesus declared he longed to do for Jerusalem and, by implication, for all Israel. But, at the moment, all he could see were chicks scurrying off in the opposite direction, taking no notice of the smoke and flames indicating the approach of danger, nor of the urgent warnings of the one who alone could give them safety.

This picture of the hen and the chickens is a strong statement of what Jesus thought his death would be all about. But before we examine it further, we should go back to the earlier part of the passage. If chicks are in mind then the other great danger alongside fire was the predator, particularly the fox. And that's the image Jesus uses for Herod.

For most of the gospel story, Herod has cast a dark shadow across the page, but he has not until now posed an explicit threat to Jesus. The Pharisees here, who warn Jesus of Herod's intentions, may have been among the many moderate Pharisees who, like Gamaliel in Acts 5, were happy to watch from the sidelines and see whether or not this new movement turned out to be from God. They may, of course, have been secretly hoping to get rid of Jesus, to get him off their territory; but Luke gives no hint of that if it was so. What is more important is Jesus' answer.

Jesus clearly indicates his contempt for Herod. Everyone knew, after all, that his only claim to royalty was because the Romans, recognizing his father as the most effective thug around, had promoted him from nowhere to keep order at the far end of their territories. Jesus also strongly affirms his own strange vocation: yes, he will eventually die at the hands of the authorities, but no, it won't be in Galilee. Herod will have an indirect hand in it (Luke 23.6–12), but he remains a minor player.

What matters is that Jesus has a destiny to fulfil. He is to go to Jerusalem and die, risking the threats of the fox, and adopting the role of the mother hen to the chickens faced with sudden danger. But will Jerusalem benefit from his offer? Jerusalem has a long history of rebelling against God, refusing the way of peace (that sentence, alas, seems to be as true in the modern as in the ancient world). As Ezekiel saw, rebellion meant that the holy presence of God had abandoned the Temple and the city, opening the way for devastating enemy attack (Ezekiel 10—11). The only way for the city and Temple to avoid the destruction which now threatened them was to welcome Jesus as God's peace-envoy; but all the signs were that they would not.

Israel's greatest crisis is coming upon her, and Jesus is offering an urgent summons to repent, to come his kingdom way, his way of peace. This is the only way of avoiding the disaster which will otherwise follow her persistent rebellion. Jesus' intention now, in obedience to his vocation, is to go to Jerusalem and, like the hen with the chickens, to take upon himself the full force of that disaster which he is predicting for the nation and the Temple. The one will give himself on behalf of the many.

For reflection or discussion

- Reflect on the powerful imagery of the hen gathering her chicks under her wings in the context of Jesus' longing to protect

Jerusalem. Think about the significance of sacrifice and selfless-ness portrayed in this image and how it relates to Jesus' ultimate sacrifice on the cross.

• Reflect on the invitation to repentance and the way of peace that Jesus offers. What are the consequences of accepting or rejecting this invitation?

Tuesday

The triumphal entry: Luke 19.28–40

[28]Jesus went on ahead, going up to Jerusalem.

[29]As they came close, as near as Bethany and Bethphage, at the place called the Mount of Olives, he sent two of the disciples on ahead. [30]'Go into the village over there,' he said, 'and as you arrive you'll find a colt tied up, one that nobody has ever ridden. Untie it and bring it here. [31]If anyone says to you, "Why are you untying it?" you should say, "Because the master needs it."'

[32]The two who were sent went off and found it just as Jesus had said to them. [33]They untied the colt, and its owners said to them, 'Why are you untying the colt?'

[34]'Because the master needs it,' they replied.

[35]They brought it to Jesus, threw their cloaks on the colt, and mounted Jesus on it. [36]As he was going along, people kept spreading their cloaks on the road.

[37]When he came to the descent of the Mount of Olives, the whole crowd of disciples began to celebrate and praise God at the tops of their voices for all the powerful deeds they had seen.

[38]'Welcome, welcome, welcome with a blessing,' they sang.

'Welcome to the king in the name of the Lord!

'Peace in heaven, and glory on high!'

[39]Some of the Pharisees from the crowd said to Jesus, 'Teacher, tell your disciples to stop that.'

⁴⁰'Let me tell you,' replied Jesus, 'if they stayed silent, the stones would be shouting out!'

Mile after uphill mile, it seems a long way even today in a car. You wind up through the sandy hills from Jericho, the lowest point on the face of the earth, through the Judaean desert, climbing all the way. Halfway up, you reach sea level; you've already climbed a long way from the Jordan valley, and you still have to ascend a fair-sized mountain. It is almost always hot; since it seldom if ever rains, it's almost always dusty as well.

That was the way the pilgrims came, with Jesus going on ahead, as he had planned all along. This was to be the climax of his story, of his public career, of his vocation. He knew well enough what lay ahead, and had set his face to go and meet it head on. He couldn't stop announcing the kingdom, but that announcement could only come true if he now embodied in himself the things he'd been talking about. The living God was at work to heal and save, and the forces of evil and death were massed to oppose him, like Pharaoh and the armies of Egypt trying to prevent the Israelites from leaving. But this was to be the moment of God's new Exodus, God's great Passover, and nothing could stop Jesus going ahead to celebrate it.

Even when you drive, rather than walk, from Jericho to the top of the Mount of Olives, the sense of relief and excitement when you reach the summit is intense. At last you exchange barren, dusty desert for lush green growth, particularly at Passover time, at the height of spring. At last you stop climbing, you crest the summit, and there before you, glistening in the sun, is the holy city, Jerusalem itself, on its own slightly smaller hill across a narrow but deep valley. Bethany and Bethphage nestle on the Jericho side of the Mount of Olives. Once you pass them, Jerusalem comes into view almost at once. The end of the journey; the pilgrimage to end all pilgrimages; Passover time in the city of God.

For Jesus it's a royal occasion, to be carefully planned and staged so as to make exactly the right point. The animal he chose – presumably by pre-arrangement with the owners; this wasn't the first time Jesus had been to Bethany! – was a young foal, almost certainly a donkey's colt. (The word Luke uses would more normally mean a young horse or pony; but he knew Zechariah 9.9, the prophecy of the Messiah riding on a young donkey, and he uses the word that occurs there.) Like the tomb in which Jesus would lie a week later (23.52), it had never been used before. The disciples pick up the theme, and in a kind of instant royal celebration they spread cloaks along the road for him. Down they go, down the steep path to the Kidron valley, and the crowd starts to sing part of the great psalm of praise (Psalm 118) that pilgrims always sang on the way to Jerusalem: a song of victory, a hymn of praise to the God who defeats all his foes and establishes his kingdom. Jesus will himself quote from the psalm in one of his debates in Jerusalem (20.17). He comes himself as the fulfilment of the nation's hopes, answering their longings for a king who would bring peace to earth from heaven itself.

And yet . . . the grumblers are still there; some Pharisees, going along with the crowd, suddenly become anxious about what will happen if the authorities in Jerusalem think for a minute that there's a messianic demonstration going on. Jesus knows, and Luke knows, and we as his readers know, what awaits the master when he gets to the city. From Jesus' point of view, this is why there is such a celebration in the first place: it is appropriate precisely because he is coming to bring God's salvation, God's great Exodus, through his own Passover action on the cross. Had the crowds known this, they would have been puzzled and distressed, as indeed they soon will be.

For reflection or discussion

- Explore the tension between the triumphant atmosphere of Jesus' entry into Jerusalem and the underlying knowledge of his impending suffering and death. Reflect on the reactions of different groups, such as the disciples, the crowd and the Pharisees.

What were the different levels of awareness and understanding regarding Jesus' mission?

- Imagine you are arriving at Jerusalem with Jesus. Are you going along for the trip in the hope that Jesus will fulfil some of your hopes and desires? Are you ready to sing a psalm of praise, but only as long as Jesus seems to be doing what you want? Are you ready not only to spread your cloak on the road in front of him, to do the showy and flamboyant thing, but also to follow him into trouble and adversity?

Wednesday

Jesus cleanses the Temple: Luke 19.41–48

[41]When Jesus came near and saw the city, he wept over it.

[42]'If only you'd known,' he said, 'on this day – even you! – what peace meant. But now it's hidden, and you can't see it. [43]Yes, the days are coming upon you when your enemies will build up earthworks all round you, and encircle you, and squeeze you in from every direction. [44]They will bring you crashing to the ground, you and your children within you. They won't leave one single stone on another, because you didn't know the moment when God was visiting you.'

[45]He went into the Temple and began to throw out the traders. [46]'It's written,' he said, 'my house shall be a house of prayer; but you've made it a brigands' cave.'

[47]He was teaching every day in the Temple. But the chief priests, the scribes and the leading men of the people were trying to destroy him. [48]They couldn't find any way to do it, because all the people were hanging on his every word.

At last it is Jesus' turn to cry. Earlier in the Gospel of Luke we find other people in tears and others in distress coming to him for healing and new life. But Jesus is not immune to tears. In John's gospel,

Jesus weeps at the tomb of his friend Lazarus (John 11.35). Now here he weeps over the city, and there is no one to console him.

Jesus' tears are at the core of the Christian gospel. This was not a moment of regrettable weakness, something a real Messiah ought to have avoided. Again and again during his long journey he had warned of God's impending judgment on the city and Temple, because they, like the towns of Galilee, had resisted his call for peace, for the gospel of God's grace which would reach out in love to the Gentile world. Unless you repent, he said, you will all likewise perish (13.3, 5); now here he was, face to face with the city where Pilate had killed Galileans and would shortly kill one more, face to face with the city where the tower of Siloam had fallen and where, before too long, towers and walls and the Temple itself would come crashing down.

It is an essential part of Jesus' message of warning and judgment that it is uttered, finally, through sobs and tears. Luke's writing of the scene is vivid, conveying the sense of Jesus sobbing out a few phrases, until he finally controls himself sufficiently to utter the solemn warning upon the city that has chosen to ignore the moment when God was coming in solemn 'visitation'.

There is no sense of 'I told you so' or 'It serves you right'; only the shaking sobs of the prophet like Jeremiah. The terrible judgment that has been pronounced, and will shortly be executed, proceeds not from a stern and cold justice but from a heart of love that wants the best for, and from, the people, and so must now oppose, with sorrow and tears, the rebellion that has set its own interests and agendas before those of the God who established them there in the first place.

The tears and the Temple action, then, go together. Jesus is not simply mounting an angry protest about the commercialization of Temple business. His action is a solemn prophetic warning, echoing those of Jeremiah and others, that if the Temple becomes a hide-out for brigands, literally or metaphorically, it will come under God's judgment. Now, it appears, the brigands are indeed running the show. Jesus is not so much concerned with the traders; they, to be sure, are doubtless making a few extra shekels on the side, but that's trivial compared with what the high priests and their entourage have been doing.

The Temple had become the focal point of the national ideology. As in Isaiah's day, it stood in the public imagination for the unshakeable promise of Israel's God to keep Israel safe, come what may. And, as in Isaiah's day, Israel had to face the challenge that unless the promise was met with faith and obedience it would count for nothing, and indeed worse than nothing; it would turn into a curse. If you're in covenant with the holy God, disobedience doesn't simply prevent blessings, bringing you back, as it were, to square one. It calls down the judgment that a sorrowful God will pour out on his people when they reject him and his purposes.

Not surprisingly, the message was unpopular with the ruling group, clerical and lay. Jesus' action in the Temple was the immediate cause of his arrest. But behind what he did, and how the rulers reacted, was the whole weight of his previous ministry. As the storm clouds gather, we sense the inevitability which Luke in any case highlights frequently: this was how it 'must' be. This is how God's plan of salvation must be accomplished.

For reflection or discussion

- Consider the role of tears and sorrow in Jesus' ministry. How is God's love and justice manifested in Jesus' actions and teachings?
- What role does Jesus' Temple action play in the larger context of his ministry and God's plan of salvation? Reflect on the inevitable course of events that leads to Jesus' arrest and crucifixion.

Thursday

A question about Jesus' authority: Luke 20.1–8

[1]On one of those days, while Jesus was teaching the people in the Temple, and announcing the good news, the chief priests

and the scribes came up with the elders, and said to him, ²'Tell us: by what authority are you doing these things? Or who gave you this authority?'

³'I've got a question for you, too,' said Jesus, 'so tell me this: ⁴was John's baptism from God, or was it merely human?'

⁵'If we say it was from God,' they said among themselves, 'he'll say, So why didn't you believe him? ⁶But if we say "merely human", all the people will stone us, since they're convinced that John was a prophet.'

⁷So they replied that they didn't know where John and his baptism came from.

⁸'Very well, then,' said Jesus. 'Neither will I tell you by what authority I do these things.'

There was once a debate in Britain about how loud soldiers should shout while on parade. The army was anxious, it seems, that sooner or later a soldier would suffer damaged hearing because a sergeant major had bellowed an order at high volume and at close range. The newspapers, naturally, thought this was ridiculous. Orders have to be heard. It's no use whispering on the field of battle.

At the same time, a sergeant major receives orders from more senior officers, and they do not normally shout. In fact, the further up the ranks you go, the less likely are the orders to make any noise: the commanding officer may simply write down his instructions, or speak them in a quiet voice to his next in command. So if someone were to come to a parade ground or army barracks and try to discover who was in command, and where they got their authority from, it wouldn't be much good assuming that the loudest voice meant the most important authority.

We might have forgotten John the Baptist by this stage of the gospel story, but Luke hasn't, because Jesus hasn't. When Jesus came into Jerusalem and threw the traders out of the Temple, he was acting like someone who thinks he's in charge. But there already was an authority structure in the Temple, a pyramid with guards at the bottom and the chief priests at the top, with the high priest himself as the most senior figure. Who does Jesus think he is to come in, without any accreditation, and start throwing his weight about? That is the natural question to ask.

But Jesus' answer, which seems to take them by surprise, must not have seemed natural at all. What has John got to do with Jesus? Is this just (as their whispered debate among themselves seems to suggest they think) a trick question to catch them out and make them look foolish in the eyes of the people?

Not at all. The reason Jesus asks the question is because the authority he has over the Temple is precisely his royal, messianic authority; and his royal status and authority was conferred on him publicly at the time of John's baptism, with the descent of the dove and the voice from heaven. If John was a true prophet, then Jesus is indeed the true Messiah, with authority over the Temple, because he was marked out as such as he came up out of the water. If, of course, John was not a true prophet – if he was simply a dangerous dreamer, leading people astray – then Jesus, too, may be acting out of line (as the authorities obviously think, but dare not say).

Authority is therefore passing, quietly and without many people noticing, from the old system to the new. For Luke, writing with half an eye at least on the Roman Empire, this is enormously important. Jesus, for him, is the Lord of the world, the one before whom Caesar himself ought to shiver in his shoes; how much more is he Lord of the Temple and all that is in it? The high priest may make the loudest noise in Jerusalem, with his henchmen and his court, his access to the Roman governor, and the prestige that comes with his ceremonial and political role. But now his power is challenged by one who speaks more quietly, one who comes with prophetic and royal authority that challenges the old regime and introduces the new. From now on – even as he hangs on the cross that marked Caesar's rule, mocked by the same chief priests! – Jesus will exercise that authority, the powerful authority of saving and healing love, until all acknowledge it.

We today, living out beyond the rule of Caesar and the chief priests, may find it quite a complex business to come to terms with the authority of Jesus. We should of course, as Christians, acknowledge him as sovereign of our lives, our thoughts and actions, and seek to live under that authority, even when it comes (as it often does) in whispers rather than in a loud voice. But if Jesus is master or Lord of the whole world, as Luke certainly believed, we have the task of making that lordship known.

For reflection or discussion

- What is the difference between authority based on power and loud voices and authority based on prophetic calling? How does Jesus' authority as the Messiah challenge the religious leaders and their understanding of authority within the Temple?
- Think about how we witness to the authority of Jesus today. Normally it won't be appropriate to overturn tables and expel people from buildings! What symbolic actions will be appropriate in our world, to make the point that Jesus possesses all authority in heaven and on earth?

Friday

Watching for the son of man: Luke 21.34–38

[34]'Watch out for yourselves,' said Jesus. 'Don't let your hearts grow heavy with dissipation and drunkenness and the cares of this life, letting that day come upon you suddenly, [35]like a trap. It will come, you see, on everyone who lives on the face of the earth. [36]Keep awake at all times, praying that you may have strength to escape all these things that will happen, and to stand before the son of man.'

³⁷Jesus was teaching in the Temple by day, but at night he went out and stayed in the place called the Mount of Olives. ³⁸From early morning all the people flocked to him in the Temple, to hear him.

Travel with me, back in time, to Jerusalem. The year is AD 58, nearly thirty years after Jesus' crucifixion and resurrection. Many people in the holy city came to believe in Jesus in the heady days nearly a generation ago, and many of them are still here, older and more puzzled perhaps, but still waiting and hoping and praying.

Things have been difficult, on and off. Once Pontius Pilate stopped being governor people hoped life might improve, but there was then a huge crisis over the emperor's plan to place a vast statue of himself in the Temple. The threat, fortunately, was seen off; Gaius, the emperor in question, had died soon after; and when one of Herod's grandsons, Agrippa, was made king of the Jews in 41 everyone in Jerusalem stood up and cheered. To be ruled by one of your own might be better than having governors from far away who didn't understand local customs. That didn't last, though. He too had died, struck down (said some) by God for blasphemously claiming the sort of divine honours that his pagan masters had given themselves. Now there had been a string of new Roman governors, each one (it seemed) worse than the last. But in 54, when Nero became emperor, many people hoped again that peace and justice would triumph.

All along, though, people in Jerusalem were aware of the political tensions building up. Revolutionary movements arose, had their moment of glory, and were brutally crushed. Some said the priests were secretly involved. Some said it was all the wicked brigands, refusing to let ordinary people go about their business in peace. Some wanted an easy-going peace with Rome, others were all for driving hard bargains, others again wished the Messiah would come. Daily life went on: buying and selling, growing crops, tending herds, woodwork, leatherwork, money-changing, pottery, with the daily round of Temple sacrifices, music, celebrations and the seasonal feasts as the constant backdrop. The Temple itself was almost complete: the programme of rebuilding begun by Herod the Great seventy years earlier was finally drawing to a close.

And in the middle of all this, those who named the name of Jesus, who still met to break bread and worship in his name, and to teach one another the stories of what he'd done and said, were pulled and pushed this way and that. Some of them were friends of the ex-Pharisee Saul of Tarsus, now known as Paul. He had been here not long ago, and had caused a riot (his friends said his opponents had caused it, but the word on the street was that riots tended to happen wherever Paul went). Now he'd gone, sent to Rome for trial, and he wouldn't be back. Peter, too, had gone on his travels and hadn't been seen for years. Others were sceptical of Paul; he had compromised God's law, they said, allowing Gentiles to worship God through Jesus without demanding circumcision. The leader of the Jerusalem Christians, the wise and devout James, the brother of Jesus himself, was getting older, and his prayers for the redemption of his people didn't seem to be answered.

How easy it was for Jerusalem Christians to become weary! If the gospel was producing exciting results, it was doing so across the sea, and they only heard about it every once in a while, and didn't always like what they heard (Gentiles claiming to worship Jesus but not keeping the law of Moses – that sort of thing). Their lives dragged on day by day. Friends asked them, sometimes unkindly, when this Messiah of theirs was going to reappear, and could he please hurry up because much more of these Romans banging around would bring on a world war, and anyway look what had happened to the price of bread, and if Jesus had really been the Messiah why had nothing much happened since? Not much use to say that when you met for worship the sense of Jesus' presence and love was so real you could almost reach out and touch him. Not much of an answer to say that you had been told to be patient. Thirty years is a long time. All you can do is retell the stories, including the sayings of Jesus such as you find in this passage. Hang on. Be alert. Prop your eyes open – physically, perhaps; spiritually for sure. Pray for strength to meet whatever comes. The son of man will be vindicated, and when he is you want to be on your feet.

Now travel with me to San Francisco, or Sydney, or Bujumbura, or San Salvador, in the twenty-first century. You emerge from the church on Sunday morning – the Pentecostal celebration, the Anglican Matins, the Spanish Mass – and there is the world going about its business, or as it may be its pleasure. Your friends think you're odd still going to church. Everybody knows Christianity is outdated, disproved, boring and irrelevant. What you need is more sex; more parties; more money-making; more revolution. Anyway, hasn't the church done some pretty bad things in its time? What about the Inquisition? (They always say that.) What about the Crusades? Who needs Christianity now that we have computers and space travel? (They said it before about electricity and modern medicine.)

And anyway, they say, if your Jesus is so special, why is the world still in such a mess? They don't want to know about the freeing of the slaves, the rise of education and the building of hospitals; they certainly don't want to know about the lives that are changed every day by the gospel. They want to load you with the cares of this life; and, as Jesus warned, with dissipation and drunkenness, literal and metaphorical. They want to wear you down, to make you think you're odd and stupid. Why study an old book, they say, that's never done anyone any good?

The answer is the same for us as it was for the Jerusalem Christians nearly a generation after Jesus. Keep alert. This is what you were told to expect. Patience is the key. Pray for strength to keep on your feet. There will be times when your eyes shut with tiredness, spiritual, mental, emotional and physical, and when you will have to prop them open. This is what it's about: not an exciting battle, with adrenalin flowing and banners flying, but the steady tread, of prayer

and hope and scripture and sacrament and witness, day by day and
week by week. This is what counts; this is why patience is a fruit of
the spirit. Read the story again. Remind one another of what Jesus
said. And keep awake.

For reflection or discussion

• Consider the role of patience in your spiritual journey. Reflect
on the importance of waiting and enduring, even when it seems
as if nothing is changing or progressing. How can you cultivate
patience in your relationship with God and in your interactions
with others? How does patience contribute to your spiritual
growth?

• We live in an age when many view Christianity as outdated or
irrelevant. How does gathering with other believers for worship,
prayer and study help you to stay alert and steadfast? How can
you encourage and support fellow believers in their own faith
journeys?

Saturday

The Last Supper: Luke 22.1–23

[1]The time came for the festival of unleavened bread, known as
Passover. [2]The chief priests and the scribes looked for a way to
assassinate Jesus, a difficult task because of the crowds.

[3]The satan entered into Judas, whose surname was Iscariot,
who was one of the company of the Twelve. [4]He went and held
a meeting with the chief priests and officers, to discuss how he
might hand Jesus over. [5]They were delighted, and promised to
pay him. [6]He agreed, and started to look for an opportunity
to hand him over to them when the crowds weren't around.

[7]The day of unleavened bread arrived, the day when people
had to kill the Passover lamb. [8]Jesus dispatched Peter and John.

'Off you go,' he said, 'and get the Passover ready for us to eat.'
⁹'Where d'you want us to prepare it?' they asked him.

¹⁰'Listen carefully,' said Jesus. 'As you go into the city a man will meet you carrying a jar of water. Follow him, and when he goes into a house, go after him. ¹¹Then say to the householder there, "The teacher says, 'Where is the living-room where I can eat the Passover with my disciples?'" ¹²And he will show you a large upstairs room, laid out and ready. Make the preparations there.'

¹³So they went and found it as he had said to them, and they prepared the Passover.

¹⁴When the time came, Jesus sat down at table with the apostles.

¹⁵'I have been so much looking forward to eating this Passover with you before I have to suffer,' he said to them. ¹⁶'For – let me tell you – I won't eat it again until it's fulfilled in the kingdom of God.'

¹⁷Then he took a cup, and gave thanks, and said, 'Take this and share it among yourselves. ¹⁸Let me tell you, from now on I won't drink from the fruit of the vine until the kingdom of God comes.'

¹⁹Then he took some bread. He gave thanks, broke it and gave it to them.

'This is my body,' he said, 'which is given for you. Do this in memory of me.'

²⁰So too, after supper, with the cup: 'This cup', he said, 'is the new covenant, in my blood which is shed for you.

²¹'But look here! Someone here is going to betray me. His hand is with mine at this table. ²²The son of man is indeed going, as it is marked out for him; but woe betide that man by whom he is betrayed!'

²³They began to ask each other which of them was going to do this.

When Jesus wanted to give his followers – then and now – a way of understanding what was about to happen to him, he didn't teach them a theory.

Theories about how Jesus' death dealt with our sins have come and gone throughout church history. Many of them are profoundly moving, drawing together deep spiritual insight, remarkable theological understanding, and a commitment to bring God's saving love to the needy world. Many of them have inspired Christian people with a new view of God's grace and mercy. Theories have their proper place. But they weren't the main thing that Jesus gave his followers.

He gave them an act to perform. Specifically, he gave them a meal to share. It is a meal that speaks more volumes than any theory. The best way of finding out what it says is of course to do it, not to talk or write about it; but since this is a book, and my readers are not with me at the Lord's table, let me suggest some of the things that Jesus seems to have intended – and some of the things that Luke, in writing about it, seems to have wanted to draw out.

It was, first and foremost, a *Passover* meal. Luke has told us all along that Jesus was going to Jerusalem to 'accomplish his Exodus' (9.31). He has come to do for Israel and the whole world what God did through Moses and Aaron in the first Exodus. When the powers of evil that were enslaving God's people were at their worst, God acted to judge Egypt and save Israel. And the sign and means of both judgment and rescue was the Passover: the angel of death struck down the firstborn of all Egypt, but spared Israel as the firstborn of God, 'passing over' their houses because of the blood of the lamb on the doorposts (Exodus 12). Now the judgment that had hung over Israel and Jerusalem, the judgment Jesus had spoken of so often, was to be meted out; and Jesus would deliver his people *by taking its force upon himself.* His own death would enable his people to escape.

Escape from what? From the powers of evil. A little later Jesus spoke of the dark powers having their moment of glory (22.53). We still don't understand the nature and power of evil much better than people did in Jesus' day, but if we believe that in any sense God's plan of salvation for the world was reaching its climax in Jesus it isn't surprising that the forces of evil were doing their best to thwart it. Jesus has been going through a lifetime of 'trials' (verse 28), and the supreme one is now upon him. He will go through it so that his followers need not. They must 'eat his body' and 'drink his blood', finding their life through his death.

Jesus had been passionately looking forward to this meal. It was, for him, the moment above all when he would explain to his followers, in deeds and words rich and heavy with meaning, what he was about to do and how they could profit from it. It's no accident, therefore, that the story of the meal is interwoven with the story of betrayal. John's gospel speaks of a period after Judas left the room, in which Jesus could instruct the eleven in peace – though even then much of that instruction centred upon the coming persecution (John 13.31—17.26). In Luke's scene, Judas is there throughout, presumably slipping away unnoticed as the meal draws to a close.

At the small-scale level, Judas provided what the chief priests needed: an opportunity to arrest Jesus when there were no crowds around. (It was to avoid this danger that Jesus made secret plans for the Passover celebration.) But in Luke's understanding – and this is vital to what he sees going on at the supper itself – 'the satan' is using Judas for a purpose. The satan's purpose is always to accuse. Jesus is to be accused of being a deceiver, a rebel, a false prophet, a fake Messiah: in other words, a liar who is endangering Israel. Judas's betrayal is the first step in this process of accusation.

But Luke will tell us in a hundred ways that Jesus is in fact innocent of the charges laid against him, and that it is Israel itself that is guilty. The blend of celebration and betrayal in the scene at supper is preparing us for the blend of triumph and tragedy in the crucifixion itself. Jesus accomplishes his true mission by being falsely accused. He achieves his divine vocation by submitting to the punishment that others deserved. As God took the arrogant opposition of

Pharaoh in Egypt and made it serve his own ends in the spectacular rescue of his people, so now, through this one man at supper with his friends, we see God doing the same thing. When the powers of evil do their worst, and crucify the one who brings God's salvation, God uses that very event to defeat those powers.

We who, daily, weekly or however often, come together to obey Jesus' command to break bread and drink wine in his memory, find ourselves drawn into that salvation, that healing life. The powers may still rage, like Pharaoh and his army pursuing the Egyptians after Passover. But they have been defeated, and rescue is secure.

For reflection or discussion

- Reflect on the symbolism of judgment and rescue present in the Passover story and how it relates to Jesus' death and the defeat of the powers of evil. How does participating in the Lord's Supper reinforce your trust in God's deliverance and victory over the forces of darkness?
- Contemplate the tension between celebration and betrayal in the scene at supper and its foreshadowing of the triumph and tragedy of the crucifixion. Reflect on the sacrificial nature of Jesus' mission and his willingness to bear the punishment others deserved. How does this sacrificial love demonstrated by Jesus affect your understanding of forgiveness, redemption and God's ability to use even the darkest events for his purposes?

Holy Week
Jesus on the cross

Monday

Jesus is arrested: Luke 22.39–53

[39]Jesus headed, as usual, for the Mount of Olives, and his disciples followed him.

[40]When he came to the place, he said to them, 'Pray that you won't come into the trial.'

[41]He then withdrew from them about a stone's throw, and knelt down to pray.

[42]'Father,' he said, 'if you wish it – please take this cup away from me! But it must be your will, not mine.' [43]An angel appeared to him from heaven, strengthening him. [44]By now he was in agony, and he prayed very fervently. And his sweat became like clots of blood, falling on the ground. [45]Then he got up from praying, and came to the disciples and found them asleep because of sorrow.

[46]'Why are you sleeping?' he said to them. 'Get up and pray, so that you won't come into the trial.'

[47]While he was still speaking, a crowd appeared. The man named Judas, one of the Twelve, was leading them. He approached Jesus to kiss him, [48]but Jesus said to him, 'Judas! Are you going to betray the son of man with a kiss?'

[49]Jesus' followers saw what was about to happen.

'Master!' they said. 'Shall we go in with the swords?' [50]And one of them struck the high priest's servant, and cut off his right ear.

[51]'Enough of that!' said Jesus, and healed the ear with a touch.
[52]Then Jesus spoke to the arresting party – the chief priests, the Temple guards, and the elders.

'Anyone would think I was a brigand,' he said, 'seeing you coming out like this with swords and clubs! [53]Every day I've been in the Temple with you and you never laid hands on me. But your moment has come at last, and so has the power of darkness.'

One of the most noticeable changes in my life in the last thirty years – apart from increasing baldness – has been my changing attitude to one of the sports that I loved as a young man. I learned to rock-climb when I was at school, and for ten or more years I did as much of it as I could, never with great skill but always with huge enjoyment. But now, though I love walking in the hills, I have no desire whatever to find myself with my toes wobbling on tiny ledges and my heels suspended over a few hundred feet of fresh air.

Apart from anything else, there is a peculiarly tragic aspect to many mountaineering accidents. The rope that's supposed to save, by joining the climbers together, can also kill. However well prepared the climbers may be, it sometimes happens that when one person falls they pull the other climbers off the rock as well. One person's downfall can take the others with them.

That is what Jesus was most anxious to avoid in this passage. The disciples didn't understand what he was doing or saying, but with hindsight we can see it. He knew not only that he would be arrested, tried and killed, but that it was his God-given vocation that this should be so. But he also knew that he must go alone into the hour and power of darkness. When rebel leaders were rounded up, their associates were frequently captured, tortured and killed along with them; it was vital that this shouldn't happen to Peter and the rest. Jesus would fall, but he mustn't drag them down with him; his vocation was to give his life for the sheep, not to have them killed as well.

In any case, they were the ones who would carry his mission forward in the days to come; he had prayed for Peter particularly (22.32), and it was vital that he and the others should stay out of the process that would shortly engulf him.

That's why he tells them to pray 'that they may escape the trial'. What 'trial' is he talking about? At one level, it's the trial that Jesus knows will await him once he's arrested. But this trial will be only the human and earthly version of the greater 'trial' that is coming on Jesus, on Israel, on the whole world. 'Your moment has come,' he said to the arresting party, 'and so has the power of darkness.' Like many Jews of his day, Jesus believed that Israel's history, and with it world history, would pass into a moment of great terror and darkness, unspeakable suffering and sorrow, and that God's redemption, the coming kingdom and all that it meant, would emerge the other side. This would be the 'trial', the 'test', the 'great tribulation'. Unlike any other leaders of the day, Jesus believed that it was his appointed task to go into that darkness, that terror, all by himself, to carry the fate of Israel and the world through to the other side. He would face The Trial, in both senses, alone.

Only this explains the horror that Jesus faced in the garden. Others (Socrates, famously; thousands of martyrs, Christian and non-Christian alike, in fame or obscurity) have gone to their deaths, including horrific and agonizing ones, with apparent equanimity. Jesus had just celebrated the meal at which he had not only foretold his own death but given his own key to what it would mean. Why did he now shrink?

The best answer is that he knew this death would carry with it the full horror of darkness, of God-forsakenness. He was going to the place where the evil powers of the world could and would do their worst at every level. And part of the torture was precisely the mental agony, the insistent questioning: perhaps there would be another way, maybe he'd misread God's signals, maybe, as with Abraham when he was about to sacrifice Isaac, now that he'd come this far perhaps God would do something new which would mean he didn't have to go through with it. Luke's addition of the medical detail about Jesus sweating drops of blood has been confirmed by modern research; under conditions of extreme stress and horror, this can and does happen.

And in the middle of it, the disciples still didn't understand what Jesus' kingdom, his message of peace, was all about. Their attempts at defending him missed the point just as much as the swords and clubs of the guardsmen. He was neither a revolutionary fighter nor a military Messiah. But the time for explanations had passed. The hour of darkness had come, and nobody would see clearly again until the new dawn three days later.

For reflection or discussion

- How does Jesus' anticipation of both a human trial and a greater spiritual trial reveal his understanding of the larger cosmic battle between good and evil? How can we find strength and resilience in the face of personal and collective trials?

- Explore the profound agony Jesus experienced in the garden and his momentary hesitation. What does this reveal about the weight of the darkness and God-forsakenness he was about to endure? How does Jesus' struggle with the possibility of another way reflect the tension between human desires and divine purposes?

Tuesday

Peter denies Jesus: Luke 22.54–71

54'They arrested Jesus, took him off, and brought him into the high priest's house. Peter followed at a distance. 55'They lit a fire in the middle of the courtyard and sat around it, and Peter sat in among them.

[56]A servant-girl saw him sitting by the fire. She stared hard at him. 'This fellow was with him!' she said.

[57]Peter denied it. 'I don't know him, woman,' he said.

[58]After a little while another man saw him and said, 'You're one of them!'

'No, my friend, I'm not,' replied Peter.

[59]After the space of about an hour, another man insisted, 'It's true! This man was with him; he's a Galilean too!'

[60]'My good fellow,' said Peter, 'I don't know what you're talking about.' And at once, while he was still speaking, the cock crowed. [61]The master turned and looked at Peter, and Peter called to mind the words the master had spoken to him: 'Before the cock crows, this very day, you will deny me three times.' [62]And he went outside and wept bitterly.

[63]The men who were holding Jesus began to make fun of him and knock him about. [64]They blindfolded him.

'Prophesy!' they told him. 'Who is it that's hitting you?'

[65]And they said many other scandalous things to him.

[66]When the day broke, the official assembly of the people, the chief priests and the scribes came together, and they took him off to their council.

[67]'If you are the Messiah,' they said, 'tell us!'

'If I tell you,' he said to them, 'you won't believe me. [68]And if I ask you a question, you won't answer me. [69]But from now on the son of man will be seated at the right hand of God's power.'

[70]'So you're the son of God, are you?' they said.

'You say that I am,' he said to them.

[71]'Why do we need any more witnesses?' they said. 'We've heard it ourselves, from his own mouth!'

I was fortunate enough to be involved in a service commemorating the life and witness of Wang Zhiming. He was a Chinese pastor who, after maintaining a clear Christian witness in the days of

Mao's cultural revolution, was executed in front of a large crowd. He is one of hundreds of martyrs who, in recent memory, have given their lives for the Christian faith. Among the things people saw in him, the things that made the authorities angry, was that he went on telling the truth even when it became first costly, then dangerous, and finally almost suicidal to do so. Faith and truth, expressed with grace and dignity, are unconquerable. That's why Wang Zhiming is portrayed in a statue on the west front of Westminster Abbey, while nobody today remembers his accusers or executioners.

Luke highlights Jesus' faith and truth as he tells what happened the night Jesus was arrested. Peter denies he even knows Jesus. The soldiers play games, mocking Jesus as a false prophet at the very moment his prediction about Peter comes true. The council quiz him, not to know what he really believes but to find a way of framing a charge they can take to the Roman governor in the morning. And in the middle of it all stands the master, sorrowing over Peter, wounded by the soldiers, shaking his head over the self-serving Jewish leadership, and continuing to tell the truth.

It's a scene worth stepping into for a few moments, as we ponder what is at stake and what it all meant. Think of the fireside, that chilly April night. Loyalty has brought Peter this far, but as the night wears on tiredness is sapping his resolve. It's a familiar problem, which sometimes strikes in the middle of the night but more often strikes in the middle of someone's life, or of some great project. We sign on to follow Jesus, and we really mean it. We start work on our vocation, and we have every intention of accomplishing it. Beginnings are always exciting, if daunting; the midday heat, or the midnight weariness, can drain away our intentions, our energy, our enthusiasm. Few if any Christians will look down on Peter and despise him. Most, if not all, of us will think: yes, that's what it's like. That's what happens. Perhaps it's only when we've been there that, like Peter, we can start to live and work in a new way, no longer out of our own energy but out of a fresh, and humbling, call of God.

Now see the guardroom where Jesus is blindfolded. Some of the guards are brutal and rough, ready for any sport that comes along. Others are simply doing a job, but are unable to stand back when an ugly mood takes over. Their colleagues would think them weak, and might make them the next target for their fun. One of the things that makes a bully all the more violent is the sight of weakness; he covers up his own inner fears by mocking others.

This doesn't only happen in guardrooms with soldiers. It also happens in offices and boardrooms, in school playgrounds and restaurant kitchens. It happens wherever people forget that every single other person they deal with is a beautiful, fragile reflection of the creator God, to be respected and cherished – and that they themselves are commanded, too, to reflect this God in the world. It happens, in other words, whenever people decide to make themselves feel good by making other people feel bad. Once again, we have all known what that's like.

Finally and tragically, step into the courtroom. The council members have real power, if only as puppets of Rome. They have inherited a thousand-year tradition of believing in the God of justice, and they boast of how their nation can bring that justice to God's world. But their overmastering aim here is to get rid of Jesus at all costs. For the moment everything else is on hold. One statement from him will do, however cryptic it may be, as long as they can twist it and spin it to frame a charge. This is a familiar tactic to politicians, journalists and lawyers. Anyone with a quick mind, a ready tongue and a flexible conscience can practise it. And it creates innocent victims wherever it happens.

Someone asked me today what it means to say that Jesus died for the sins of the world. I gave a rather rambling, but I hope adequate, answer. But Luke is answering that question all through this passage. Peter's weakness, the guards' bullying, the court's perversion of justice; all this and much more put Jesus on the cross. It wasn't just a theological transaction; it was real sin, real human folly and rebellion, the dehumanized humanity that has lost its way and spat in God's face. 'They said many other scandalous things to him'; yes, and we've all done so. As Luke leads our eyes to the foot of the cross he means us to feel not just sorrow and pity, but shame.

For reflection or discussion

- How does Peter's denial of Jesus and the weariness that saps his resolve resonate with your own experiences of faltering in your faith or purpose? How can you find renewed strength and a fresh call from God when your energy and enthusiasm wane?
- Explore the dynamics of power and the mistreatment of others for personal gain. How does the scene of mocking and bullying in the guardroom reflect a failure to recognize the inherent worth and dignity of every individual? How can we cultivate a mind-set that values and respects others, countering the temptation to make ourselves feel superior by making others feel inferior?

Wednesday

Jesus before Pilate and Herod: Luke 23.1–12

¹The whole crowd of them got up and took Jesus to Pilate.

²They began to accuse him. 'We found this fellow', they said, 'deceiving our nation! He was forbidding people to give tribute to Caesar, and saying that he is the Messiah – a king!'

³So Pilate asked Jesus, 'You are the king of the Jews?'

'You said it,' replied Jesus.

⁴'I find no fault in this man,' said Pilate to the chief priests and the crowds. ⁵But they became insistent.

'He's stirring up the people,' they said, 'teaching them throughout the whole of Judaea. He began in Galilee, and now he's come here.'

⁶When Pilate heard that, he asked if the man was indeed a Galilean. ⁷When he learned that he was from Herod's

jurisdiction he sent him to Herod, who happened also to be in Jerusalem at that time.

⁸When Herod saw Jesus he was delighted. He had been wanting to see him for quite some time now, since he'd heard about him, and had hoped to see him perform some sign or other. ⁹He questioned him this way and that, but Jesus gave no answer at all. ¹⁰The chief priests and the scribes stood by, accusing him vehemently. ¹¹Herod and his soldiers treated Jesus with contempt; they ridiculed him by dressing him up in a splendid robe, and sent him back to Pilate. ¹²And so it happened, that very day, that Herod and Pilate became friends with each other. Up until then, they had been enemies.

Many plays, many novels, and many real-life episodes reach a climax when two people, long separated, come together at last, for good or ill. 'We meet at last, Mr Bond!' declares the villain with an ugly smile, believing he finally has the secret agent in his power. Characters in plays from Aeschylus to Shakespeare and beyond stare at one another: 'Can it really be you?' they exclaim. 'It's so good to see you at last!' we declare as a pen-friend or distant cousin steps off the plane. We will not understand Luke's scene between Jesus and Herod unless we sense that quality in it. Herod has been in the background throughout the gospel. Only Luke tells us that he had wanted to hunt Jesus down and kill him much earlier, during Jesus' Galilean ministry (13.31); only Luke now gives us this scene where they meet at last, the present and precarious 'king of the Jews' face to face with the real and coming king. Herod had longed for this moment. He saw Jesus as a combination of John the Baptist, who had fascinated him with his talk but frightened him with his warnings, and the kind of circus artiste who can do magic stunts to order.

Jesus disappoints him. He says nothing, and does no miracles. We might have expected that, like Moses at the court of Pharaoh, the leader of the new Exodus would either threaten Herod with God's judgment or perform remarkable feats to demonstrate his claims, but Jesus does neither. He isn't that sort of prophet, and he isn't that sort of king. Luke, for whom Jesus is certainly both a true prophet and the true king of the Jews, places this meeting in a sequence of scenes designed to reveal the truth of this kingship and the falsehood of all other types. At this moment, the truth is more eloquently stated by silence.

Why then did Pilate say that Jesus was innocent of the charges laid against him? Why did Herod noticeably not accede to the chief priests' accusations? Partly, it seems, because it was obvious that Jesus was not leading the sort of revolution normally spearheaded by would-be 'kings of the Jews'. His few close followers were only lightly armed, and had in any case run away. Jesus made no threats, offered no resistance, and said hardly anything. They could see that the main reason he was before them was that the chief priests and their associates wanted to get rid of him – and both Herod and Pilate disliked them and tried to do them down, as part of the power struggles that dribbled on throughout this period. Once again, Jesus was caught at the point where competing interests and agendas met. Not only the sins, but also the petty aspirations of the world conspired to put him on the cross.

But if it's important for Luke that Jesus and Herod meet at last, it is still more important that the true Lord of the world meets the representative of the political lord of the world. Luke's readers know that Jesus hasn't in fact forbidden people to give tribute to Caesar, but it was a plausible charge for one who, by speaking of his exaltation as the son of man (22.69), showed that he saw himself as the rightful and royal representative of Israel. If he was the king of the Jews, and would be elevated as king over all earthly powers, then Caesar too would be pushed down from his throne.

There is a wonderful irony to the newfound friendship of the Jewish king and the Gentile ruler. Luke's whole book has spoken of the gospel reaching out into the lands beyond – beyond official Judaism, beyond the racial and geographical boundaries of Israel, beyond prejudice and blindness – bringing together Jew and Gentile, young and old, the hated Samaritan, the tax-collector. Now, even without believing in Jesus, Herod and Pilate are reconciled. It is as though, with Jesus on the way to the cross, reconciliation cannot help breaking out all over the place.

There is, of course, no real comparison between the shady deal struck between the petty princeling and the scheming governor, and the rich fellowship in the gospel enjoyed by Jewish and Gentile believers. But Luke is alert, and wants us to be too, for every sign that the world is becoming a new place through Jesus and his crucifixion. If even Herod and Pilate can become friends through this, he says to both his church and ours, think how you too could be reconciled with anyone at all, once you both come under the shadow of the cross.

For reflection or discussion

- Consider the portrayal of Jesus and Herod's meeting in the passage. Why do you think Jesus chose silence and non-action instead of asserting his power or performing miracles? What does this teach you about true leadership and the nature of power? How can you apply this understanding to your own interactions with others?
- Even Herod and Pilate, despite their differences and conflicting interests, found a form of reconciliation through the shadow of the cross. How can the transformative power of forgiveness and understanding be applied to promote healing and unity in your relationships and communities?

Thursday

Pilate is pressured by the crowds: Luke 23.13–26

[13]Pilate called the chief priests, the rulers and the people.

[14]'You brought this man before me,' he said to them, 'on the grounds that he was leading the people astray. Look here,

then: I examined him in your presence and I found no evidence in him of the charges you're bringing against him. ¹⁵Nor did Herod; he sent him back to me. Look: there is no sign that he's done anything to deserve death. ¹⁶So I'm going to flog him and let him go.'*

¹⁸'Take him away!' they shouted out all together. 'Release Barabbas for us!' ¹⁹(Barabbas had been thrown into prison because of an uprising that had taken place in the city, and for murder.) ²⁰Pilate spoke to them again, with the intention of letting Jesus go, ²¹but they shouted back, 'Crucify him! Crucify him!'

²²'Why?' he said for the third time. 'What's he done wrong? I can't find anything he's done that deserves death, so I'm going to beat him and let him go.'

²³But they went on shouting out at the tops of their voices, demanding that he be crucified; and eventually their shouts won the day. ²⁴Pilate gave his verdict that their request should be granted. ²⁵He released the man they asked for, the one who'd been thrown into prison because of rebellion and murder, and gave Jesus over to their demands.

²⁶As they led him away, they grabbed a man from Cyrene called Simon, who was coming in to the city from the countryside, and they forced him to carry the crossbeam behind Jesus.

Shakespeare peopled his plays, as Charles Dickens did his novels, with fascinating minor characters. Each has his or her own tale to tell; none is a mere cardboard figure. Even the bear in *A Winter's Tale* is important.

Among the Evangelists, Luke has the most interesting cast of minor characters, and two of them come into focus here: Barabbas, and Simon of Cyrene. Together they help Luke tell us not only what happened to Jesus, but why it happened and what it means for us.

---

* There is no verse 17.

We need to think into their own life stories, to see the tragic day unfold from their perspective, and to learn from them both.

Barabbas was not a common criminal. Luke informs us that he had been thrown into prison for his part in a violent rebellion that had taken place in Jerusalem. This is all we know about this particular rebellion, since the non-Christian historian Josephus doesn't mention another uprising at this time; we can assume that such events were a regular occurrence, and that in the ancient world (as, alas, in the modern) the Middle East was a place where political and social frustration would regularly spill over into violence, sometimes focused on particular targets, sometimes mindless and born of the apparent hopelessness of the cause. It was, of course, because of such events that both the Romans and the chief priests were nervous of popular or messianic movements, not least at the time of major festivals. We know about Barabbas, but we must assume that he was only one of many rebel leaders in the period. He escaped crucifixion that Passover time, but the cross claimed many, perhaps dozens or even hundreds, even when no major disturbance had taken place.

Luke describes the event in such a way that we can hardly miss the point. Barabbas is guilty of some of the crimes of which Jesus, though innocent, is charged: stirring up the people, leading a rebellion. We don't know whether he saw himself, or whether his followers saw him, as a possible 'king of the Jews', but that is not unlikely. One of them is to die, and it turns out to be Jesus. Luke does not explain, as Mark and Matthew do, the custom Pilate used to release one prisoner for the crowds to celebrate the holiday, but it is clear that things come down to a choice. Either Barabbas or Jesus must die; either the one who stands for violent revolution, which Jesus has opposed from the beginning, or the one who has offered and urged the way of peace. Jesus ends up dying the death appropriate for the violent rebel. He predicted that he would be 'reckoned with the lawless' (22.37), and it has happened all too soon.

Luke's readers are by now used to seeing Jesus in company with tax-collectors and sinners. We have been told, from many angles and with many parables, that this was the appropriate and necessary focus of his ministry, embodying the outstretched love of God to all in need, going in search of lost sheep wherever they might be found. We were not, perhaps, quite prepared for it to end like this. It is one thing for Jesus to go in to eat with a man who is a sinner (19.7). It is a considerable step beyond that for him to go off and die the death of the violent rebel.

But this is in fact the climax and focus of the whole gospel. This is the point for which Luke has been preparing us all along. All sinners, all rebels, all the human race are invited to see themselves in the figure of Barabbas; and, as we do so, we discover in this story that Jesus comes to take our place, under condemnation for sins and wickednesses great and small. In the strange justice of God, which overrules the unjust 'justice' of Rome and every human system, God's mercy reaches out where human mercy could not, not only sharing, but in this case substituting for, the sinner's fate.

It is because of this that the call goes out, once we realize what Jesus is doing, for each of us to take up our own cross and follow him. This is of course where the call to Simon comes in. He had come on pilgrimage to Jerusalem from one of the Jewish communities in North Africa (the shores of the eastern Mediterranean were covered with Greek and Roman settlements, and in most there was a sizeable Jewish community), and found himself a pilgrim in a very different sense. Criminals on their way to execution normally carried the cross-piece of their own cross, as part of the shame and torture of the whole experience. Luke does not explain why Jesus was unable to carry it for himself, but it takes little imagination to fill in the blank. The previous twenty-four hours had exhausted him, and he could barely stagger through the streets to the western gate. On several occasions in the gospel Jesus has urged his followers to take up their cross and follow him. Here at last someone is doing so, and even more: carrying Jesus' own cross, Simon becomes the model for all those who, in devotion, holiness and service, tread behind Jesus on the road of humility, pain and even death.

Though Barabbas and Simon are the key to this passage, we should once more notice the crowds, and sorrowfully identify with them. The mixture of disappointment at a failed messianic movement, and fear of what might now happen if the Romans or the chief priests regarded them as supportive of its leader, drove the mob to make what all history has regarded as the wrong choice. At the same time, Luke was well aware of God's overruling of this, too, for the purposes of salvation. God turns even human wrath and mistakes to serve his plans.

And, as we reflect on the role of the small parts within Luke's large drama, we should remind ourselves that our own parts, small though they may seem, may also contribute substantially to the work of the gospel as it goes forwards. Neither Barabbas nor Simon dreamed, that day, that their names would be known, and their stories told around the world, two thousand years hence. How much more, when we follow this Jesus and carry his cross, can we be sure that God will use our small labours and sufferings within his larger work.

For reflection or discussion

- Contemplate the significance of Simon of Cyrene's act of carrying Jesus' cross. How can you emulate Simon's example in your own life by carrying the burdens of others and walking in humility and selflessness?
- The crowds that pressurized Pilate to condemn Jesus were driven by disappointment and fear. How does this resonate with the human tendency to make choices based on popular opinion or self-preservation? Reflect on moments in your life when you have been influenced by external pressures and the importance of aligning your choices with God's purposes, even in the face of opposition or uncertainty.

Good Friday

The crucifixion: Luke 23.27–49

[27]A great crowd of the people followed Jesus, including women who were mourning and wailing for him. [28]Jesus turned and spoke to them.

'Daughters of Jerusalem,' he said, 'don't cry for me. Cry for yourselves instead! Cry for your children! [29]Listen: the time is coming when you will say, "A blessing on the barren! A blessing on wombs that never bore children, and breasts that never nursed them!" [30]At that time people will start to say to the mountains, "Fall on us", and to the hills, "Cover us"! [31]Yes: if this is what they do with the green tree, what will happen to the dry one?'

[32]Two other criminals were taken away with him to be executed. [33]When they came to the place called The Skull, they crucified him there, with the criminals, one on his right and one on his left.

[34]'Father,' said Jesus, 'forgive them! They don't know what they're doing!'

They divided his clothes, casting lots for them.

[35]The people stood around watching. The rulers hurled abuse at him.

'He rescued others,' they said, 'let him try rescuing himself, if he really is the Messiah, God's chosen one!'

[36]The soldiers added their taunts, coming up and offering him cheap wine.

[37]'If you're the king of the Jews,' they said, 'rescue yourself!'

[38]The charge was written above him: 'This is the King of the Jews.'

[39]One of the bad characters who was hanging there began to insult him. 'Aren't you the Messiah?' he said. 'Rescue yourself – and us, too!'

⁴⁰But the other one told him off. 'Don't you fear God?' he said. 'You're sharing the same fate that he is! ⁴¹In our case it's fair enough; we're getting exactly what we asked for. But this fellow hasn't done anything out of order.

⁴²'Jesus,' he went on, 'remember me when you finally become king.'

⁴³'I'm telling you the truth,' replied Jesus, 'you'll be with me in paradise, this very day.'

⁴⁴By the time of the sixth hour, darkness came over all the land. ⁴⁵The sunlight vanished until the ninth hour. The veil of the Temple was ripped down the middle. ⁴⁶Then Jesus shouted out at the top of his voice, 'Here's my spirit, father! You can take care of it now!' And with that he died.

⁴⁷The centurion saw what happened, and praised God.

'This fellow', he said, 'really was in the right.'

⁴⁸All the crowds who had come together for the spectacle saw what happened, and they went away beating their breasts. ⁴⁹Those who knew Jesus, including the women who had followed him from Galilee, remained at a distance and watched the scene.

My first day at the lumber camp was probably the hardest. I was issued with thick leather gloves, and sent off to the first shed, where the planks arrived after the huge trees had been sliced up. The boards came out sideways on a massive conveyor belt, and had to be manhandled, in their different sizes, on to the trucks that took them to the next stage of the process. Up till this point, they were heavy and wet, partly because they were freshly cut and partly because they had arrived at the camp by being floated down the river. This conveyor system was known as the 'green chain'; this is where the 'green' lumber arrived and was dealt with.

The next stage was to dry the planks, which was done in a huge drying shed, after which they were cut again and sent to the 'dry chain', where they were sorted for shipping. That's where I ended up working for most of the time. By now the wood was about half the weight; all the moisture had been dried out of the planks, and they were easier to handle and ready for use.

The contrast between 'green' and 'dry' wood supplied Jesus with one of his darkest sayings. But if we find our way to the heart of it we will learn a lot about what he, and Luke as well, thought the cross was all about. 'If they do this,' he said, 'when the wood is green, what will happen when it's dry?' (verse 31).

Jesus wasn't a rebel leader; he wasn't 'dry wood', timber ready for burning. On the contrary, he was 'green wood': his mission was about peace and repentance, about God's reconciling kingdom for Israel and the nations. But, he is saying, if they are even doing this to him, what will they do when Jerusalem is filled with young hotheads, firebrands eager to do anything they can to create violence and mayhem? If the Romans crucify the prince of peace, what will they do to genuine warlords?

Jesus, we must realize, knows that he is dying the death of the brigand, the holy revolutionary. That is part of the point. He is bearing in himself the fate he had predicted so often for the warlike nation; the woes he had pronounced on Jerusalem and its inhabitants (e.g. 13.1–5) are coming true in him. The One is bearing the sins of the many. But if the many refuse, even now, to turn and follow him, to repent of their violence, then the fate in store for them will make his crucifixion seem mild by comparison. The judgment that Rome will mete out on them will be so severe that people will beg the earth to open and swallow them up, as the prophets had warned (Hosea 10.8).

This explains the rest of the passage about the women, including its terrifying upside-down 'beatitude'. Much earlier in the gospel Jesus had invoked God's blessing on the poor, the meek, the hungry, the mourners. Now he tells the women that they will soon invoke that same blessing on those who didn't have children, who would normally be deeply ashamed of the fact (compare 1.25). These mothers will see their own sons grow up to revolt against Rome, and will watch them suffer the fate that Rome has always inflicted on rebels. Jesus combines the clear statement of his own intention, to suffer Israel's fate on her behalf, with the clear warning, echoing the warnings throughout the gospel, for those who do not follow him.

Luke makes the same point in a different way by contrasting the two who were crucified on either side of Jesus. The one taunts, but the other expresses Luke's view of the whole scene. Jesus, once again, is dying the death appropriate for the rebel, the brigand, the criminal; he is bearing the sins of the many, innocent though he himself is.

At the heart of Luke's picture of the cross is the mocking of Jesus as king of the Jews, which draws into a single stark sketch the meaning expressed by the various characters and the small incidents elsewhere in the narrative. Jesus has stood on its head the meaning of kingship, the meaning of the kingdom itself. He has celebrated with the wrong people, offered peace and hope to the wrong people, and warned the wrong people of God's coming judgment. Now he is hailed as king at last, but in mockery. Here comes his royal cupbearer, only it's a Roman soldier offering him the sour wine that poor people drank. Here is his royal placard, announcing his kingship to the world, but it is in fact the criminal charge which explains his cruel death.

His true royalty, though, shines out in his prayer and his promise, both recorded only in Luke. Unlike traditional martyrs, who died with a curse against their torturers, Jesus prays for their forgiveness. Like a king on his way to enthronement, Jesus promises a place of honour and bliss to one who requests it. ('Paradise' in Jewish thought wasn't necessarily the final resting place, but the place of rest and refreshment before the gift of new life in the resurrection.) The prayer shows that the promise is not to be taken as meaning that the only hope is in a life after death, vital though that of course is. Forgiveness brings the life of heaven to earth, God's future into the present.

For reflection or discussion

- Contemplate the significance of Jesus bearing the fate of the nation and the sins of many through his crucifixion. How does this demonstrate the depth of his sacrificial love and his identification with humanity?
- Consider the upside-down nature of Jesus' kingship and the mockery he endured as the proclaimed 'king of the Jews'. Reflect on how Jesus' life and death challenge conventional notions of power and kingship. How does this compare with the values you prioritize in your life?

Holy Saturday

The burial of Jesus: Matthew 27.57–66

⁵⁷When evening came, a rich man from Arimathea arrived. He was called Joseph, and he, too, was a disciple of Jesus. ⁵⁸He went to Pilate and requested the body of Jesus. Pilate gave the order that it should be given to him.

⁵⁹So Joseph took the body and wrapped it in a clean linen cloth. ⁶⁰He laid it in his own new tomb, which he had carved out of the rock. Then he rolled a large stone across the doorway of the tomb, and went away.

⁶¹Mary Magdalene was there, and so was the other Mary. They were sitting opposite the tomb.

⁶²On the next day (that is, the day after Preparation Day), the chief priests and the Pharisees went as a group to Pilate.

⁶³'Sir,' they said, 'when that deceiver was still alive, we recall that he said, "After three days, I'll rise again." ⁶⁴So please give the order for the tomb to be made secure until the third day. Otherwise his disciples might come and steal him away, and then tell the people, "He's been raised from the dead!", and so the last deception would be worse than the first.'

⁶⁵'You can have a guard,' said Pilate; 'go and make it as secure as you know how.' ⁶⁶So they went and made the tomb secure, sealing the stone and putting a guard on watch.

I was never much good at chess, but I have from time to time played against some reasonably good players and I remember what it felt like. There was always a point, usually quite early on, when I simply wouldn't understand what they were doing. They would move a rook here, a knight there, the queen somewhere else, and all without apparent connection or plan. Then, a few moves later, when I thought I was about to do something really clever, one of the pieces that had innocently been moved earlier on was there, blocking my way. The mark of a good player is to anticipate the moves the opponent is going to make, and to block them before they can happen.

That is more or less exactly what Matthew is doing in describing Jesus' burial. Of course there is more to it than that: there is devotion, sorrow, awe; there is gratitude to Joseph of Arimathea for being in the right place at the right time. But in many ways the burial story is actually an anticipation of the resurrection story. Matthew is moving the necessary chess pieces into place for the game he knows will take place.

The central claim of the early church was, of course, that Jesus of Nazareth had been raised from the dead. The central claim wasn't that he was a great teacher, a powerful healer, an inspiring leader, or that he was the victim of a gross miscarriage of justice. All of those were true, but they wouldn't add up to the early Christian faith and life. The crucial fact, they believed, was that Jesus had been bodily raised to life after being well and truly dead and buried. This is what they announced to the startled world, the world of Jews and Gentiles.

And of course people laughed at them, and offered alternative explanations. He wasn't really dead, they said. Or maybe the disciples stole the body. Or maybe someone else did. Or perhaps the women went to the wrong tomb. These were all stock answers to the early

Christian message, and we may suppose that from early on stock responses were developed – which then, like the skilful chess moves, could be made in advance, before the main story was even told, to rule out the wrong answers beforehand.

So the first point is that the tomb was new, readily recognizable, and sealed with a large stone. We need to pause here for a moment, because in most cultures today people don't bury the dead in the way they did in Jesus' day. Most Jews in Palestine at that time were buried in caves, sometimes underneath the houses where they had lived. The bodies weren't put in coffins, or burnt to ashes, but wrapped in a cloth along with perfumes and spices. The body would then be put on a shelf or ledge inside the cave. Then, when the flesh had all decomposed, friends or relatives would collect the bones, fold them up neatly, and put them in a bone-box (known as an 'ossuary'). Often several bodies would be on ledges in the same tomb. In this case, as Matthew has carefully explained, the tomb was new, and there were no other bodies in it.

Grave-robbery was common in the ancient world, so many cave-tombs had huge circular stones, sometimes measuring as much as two metres in diameter, which people would roll across the mouth of the cave to prevent anyone getting in without a great struggle. This is what Joseph did. You can still see some tombs of this sort in the Middle East.

The fact that Joseph requested Jesus' body from Pilate, and that Pilate granted the request, shows well enough that Jesus was indeed dead. Roman soldiers and governors didn't go in for half-measures when it came to carrying out capital sentences. Any possibility that they had let a condemned rebel leader escape death can be left out of the question. Likewise, the fact that Jesus' main disciples had nothing to do with the whole procedure, but were in hiding, indicates well enough that they wouldn't have been in a position to steal the body. Nor, indeed, could anyone else; the chief priests, anxious to avoid such a thing, obtained a guard of Roman soldiers from Pilate. They themselves sealed the stone to make sure it wasn't moved.

There remains the question of the identification of the tomb. Matthew is careful to note that the two women who went to the tomb on Easter morning (28.1) were there on the Friday evening (27.61), and saw exactly where it was.

None of this, of course, proves that the Christian story is true. Nor does the next chapter. From the very beginning there has been room for doubt, and many have taken that option. But Matthew is concerned that the doubt be located in the right place. There was no confusion about the details of the burial. If you are going to doubt whether Jesus was raised from the dead it must be because you doubt whether the living God could or would do such a thing for Israel's Messiah, the one on whose shoulders rested the weight of the world's salvation. That is what is at stake.

As we watch the burial of Jesus, and meditate on his going before us into the tomb which is the common lot of humanity, we stand in awe once more at the thought that he, alone of all the human race, has found the way through it and out into God's new world beyond. Matthew can hardly wait, we may imagine, to take the story into the next chapter where all is revealed.

For reflection or discussion

- How does the central claim of the early church that Jesus was raised from the dead form the foundation of Christian faith and life?
- Contemplate the implications of Jesus' triumph over death and his entrance into God's new world beyond the tomb. How does his resurrection inspire awe and hope in your own life? Reflect on the profound significance of Jesus' victory over death and how it affects your understanding of salvation and the power of God.

Easter Week
Jesus in glory

Easter Day

The resurrection of Jesus: Matthew 28.1–10

[1]Dawn was breaking on the first day of the week; the sabbath was over. Mary Magdalene, and the other Mary, had come to look at the tomb, [2]when suddenly there was a great earthquake. An angel of the Lord came down from heaven. He came to the stone, rolled it away, and sat down on top of it. [3]Looking at him was like looking at lightning, and his clothes were white, like snow. [4]The guards trembled with terror at him, and became like corpses themselves.

[5]'Don't be afraid,' said the angel to the women. 'I know you're looking for Jesus, who was crucified. [6]He isn't here! He's been raised, as he said he would be! Come and see the place where he was lying – [7]and then go at once, and tell his disciples that he's been raised from the dead, and that he's going on ahead of you to Galilee. That's where you'll see him. There: I've told you.'

[8]The women scurried off quickly away from the tomb, in a mixture of terror and great delight, and went to tell his disciples. [9]Suddenly, there was Jesus himself. He met them and said, 'Greetings!' They came up to him and took hold of his feet, prostrating themselves in front of him.

[10]'Don't be afraid,' said Jesus to them. 'Go and tell my brothers that they should go to Galilee. Tell them they'll see me there.'

Everyone above a certain age, in the Western world at least, can remember where they were when they heard that President Kennedy had been assassinated. Many people in other parts of the world will be able to remember where they were and what they were doing at similar moments of great national and international crisis.

Many of us also remember clearly the precise moment when something startling and very, very good happened to us. I have a vivid memory of the telephone call, nearly thirty years ago as I write this, that told me I had been appointed to my first job, a position I had set my heart on. I remember being, for once in my life, completely lost for words; the person who had called me had to repeat what he'd said before I could eventually stammer out my thanks. I remember the dry sense in my throat as I put the telephone down and called to my wife to tell her the news. I knew that from that moment on my life was going to be different. A whole new world was opening up in front of me.

It isn't difficult to understand the mixture of terror and delight that gripped the women who had gone to the tomb that morning. Mark and Luke explain that they had brought spices, since the burial had taken place in too much of a hurry (before the start of the sabbath on Friday evening) to wrap the body in the proper way. Matthew simply says that they had come to look at the tomb. At that point in the story they seem simply to be mourners, just wanting to be there, near Jesus, to pour out their sorrow in as much peace and quiet as possible.

Peace and quiet was the last thing they got. Matthew's graveside scene is easily the most dramatic of the four: an earthquake, an angel, the guards stunned into a swoon, and messages about Jesus going on ahead to Galilee. Some think, of course, that Matthew has added some of these details to make things appear more spectacular; you might just as well say, though, that the others missed them out because, if you're telling a story like this around the world, you don't want people to laugh at the details and then think they've dismissed the event itself. For Matthew, standing within a long Jewish tradition in which angels tended to appear at great moments within God's purposes, this wasn't a problem.

The point, of course, is that what is happening is the action of God himself. The God who remained apparently silent on Good Friday is having the last word. He is answering the unspoken questions of Jesus' followers, and the spoken question of Jesus himself on the cross. And what God is doing is not just an extraordinary miracle, a display of supernatural power for its own sake, or a special favour to Jesus. What God is doing is starting something new, beginning the new world promised long ago, sending the disciples to Galilee in the first place but then, as we shall see, on to the ends of the earth and the close of the age with the news of what has happened. A whole new world was opening up in front of them.

Though they were thunderstruck with amazement and fear, there is every reason to suppose that they remembered for the rest of their lives what had happened that day. The accounts of those first few moments go back to genuine personal memory, told again and again to incredulous friends and neighbours, in the tone of voice of someone saying 'I know – I almost couldn't believe it myself! It still seems totally amazing. But this is how it was.'

Though the angel tells the women that the disciples are to go to Galilee and see Jesus there, they meet him almost at once, there near the tomb. Luke simply records appearances of Jesus in the Jerusalem area; Matthew and John record them both in Jerusalem and in Galilee. (Mark's final chapter is almost certainly broken off; in the eight verses which are left, he simply has the angels instructing the women, as here, to tell the disciples to go to Galilee to see Jesus there.) But the crucial thing is that Jesus' resurrection is not about proving some point, or offering people a new spiritual experience. It is about God's purpose that must now be fulfilled. They must see Jesus, but that seeing will be a commissioning, a commissioning to a new work, a new life, a new way of life in which everything he told them before will start to come true.

We cannot today meet Jesus in the way the women did that morning. Of course, it is a vital part of Christian belief and experience that we can and should meet Jesus in spirit, and get to know him as we worship him and learn from him. That personal and intimate relationship with the living Lord is central to what being a Christian means in practice. But we would be seriously misreading Matthew, not to mention the other gospel writers, if we thought his story was just a vivid or coded way for describing that experience. He clearly intended to write of something that had actually happened, something that had not only changed the women's hearts but had torn a hole in normal history. This event had changed the world for ever. It announced, not as a theory but as a fact, that God's kingdom had come, that the son of man had been vindicated after his suffering, and that there was dawning not just another day, another week in the history of Israel and the world, but the start of God's new age that would continue until the nations had been brought into obedience.

For reflection or discussion

- Imagine being one of the women who encountered the risen Jesus at the tomb. Contemplate the mixture of amazement and fear they experienced. How would you react if you were in their shoes? How does their encounter with the resurrected Jesus inspire awe and transform their understanding of who Jesus is and what God is doing?
- Reflect on how Jesus' resurrection inaugurates God's kingdom and marks the beginning of a new age. How does this reality shape your understanding of the Christian faith and your role in participating in God's redemptive plan for the world?

Monday

The Great Commission: Matthew 28.16–20

¹⁶The eleven disciples went off to Galilee, to the mountain where Jesus had instructed them to go. ¹⁷There they saw him, and worshipped him, though some hesitated.

¹⁸Jesus came towards them and addressed them.

'All authority in heaven and on earth', he said, 'has been given to me! ¹⁹So you must go and make all the nations into disciples. Baptize them in the name of the father, and of the son, and of the holy spirit. ²⁰Teach them to observe everything I have commanded you. And look: I am with you, every single day, to the very end of the age.'

You sometimes wonder, when listening to some of the great classical composers, whether they really know how to bring a piece to an end.

One of the most notorious is Beethoven. There are times when you think you are just coming to the end of a symphony, but the chords go crashing on and on, sounding almost 'final' but leaving room for just one more . . . and then another . . . and then another . . . until the very last one dies away and the symphony is truly complete. No doubt a serious student of music would be able to explain the purpose in it, but for many listeners it seems as though a great deal has been packed into the ending, almost as though the whole symphony is being gathered up into those last few explosive chords.

Matthew's ending is much like that. Not that it goes on longer than we expect; it is in fact quite compact. But it contains so much that we would do well to slow down in our reading of these final verses and ponder each line, indeed each phrase, to see how they gather up the whole gospel and pack it tight into the final meeting between Jesus and his followers.

The scene begins on a mountain. No surprises there: a great deal in Matthew happens on a mountain. The temptations; the Sermon on the Mount; the transfiguration; the final discourse on the Mount of Olives; and now this parting scene. Moses and Elijah met the living God on a mountain, and they have appeared in this gospel talking with Jesus; now Jesus invites his disciples to meet him, so that they can be commissioned in turn.

What does surprise us is that, according to Matthew, some of them hesitated. The word can actually mean 'doubt', though we can't be sure how much of that Matthew means here. Did they hesitate over, or doubt, whether it was truly Jesus? Or did they hesitate over, or doubt, whether they, as good Jewish monotheists, believing in YHWH as the one true God, should actually *worship* Jesus? It isn't clear.

What is clear is that the majority of them did worship Jesus, and that Matthew firmly believes this was the right reaction. On several previous occasions in the gospel he has used this word ('worship') to describe people coming reverently to Jesus. Usually it seems to mean simply that they prostrated themselves before him, adopting an attitude of reverence though not necessarily implying that they thought he was divine. (See 8.2; 9.18; 14.33; 15.25; 20.20; and indeed 28.9.) Now, however, to jump for a moment to the last line of the book, it is clear that Matthew wants us to see that in Jesus the promise of the very first chapter has been fulfilled. Jesus is the 'Emmanuel', the one in whom 'God is with us' (1.23). Now he declares that he himself is 'with you always'. The only appropriate reaction to this is indeed worship, worship of the one true God who is now, astonishingly, revealed in and as Jesus himself.

In particular, Jesus has now been given 'all authority in heaven and earth'. We recall that in the temptations the devil offered Jesus this prestige, but without exacting the price that he has now paid (4.8–10). That would have been a hollow triumph, leading to the worst tyranny imaginable. Jesus' authority as the risen one, by contrast, is the authority of the one who has defeated tyranny itself, the ultimate tyranny of death; his is the authority under which life, God's new life, can begin to flourish. Despite what many people today suppose, it is basic to the most elementary New Testament faith that Jesus is *already* ruling the whole world. That is one of the most important results of his resurrection; it is part of the meaning of messiahship, which his new life after the crucifixion has made plain.

People get very puzzled by the claim that Jesus is already ruling the world, until they see what is in fact being said. The claim is not that the world is already completely as Jesus intends it to be. The claim is that he is working to take it from where it was – under the rule not only of death but of corruption, greed and every kind of wickedness – and to bring it, by slow means and quick, under the rule of his life-giving love. And how is he doing this? Here is the shock: *through us, his followers.* The project only goes forward insofar as Jesus' agents, the people he has commissioned, are taking it forward.

Many today mock this claim just as much as they mock the resurrection itself. The church in its various forms has got so much wrong, has made so many mistakes, has let its Lord down so often, that many people, including many who love Jesus for themselves, despair of it and suppose that nothing will ever change until Jesus himself returns to sort it all out. But that isn't Matthew's belief, and it doesn't fit with what we know of Jesus' commissioning of his followers in Luke, Acts and John. It doesn't fit with Paul's vision of his task. They all agree with Matthew: those who believe in Jesus, who are witnesses to his resurrection, are given the responsibility to go and make real in the world the authority which he already has. This, after all, is part of the answer to the prayer that God's kingdom will come on earth as in heaven. If we pray that prayer, we shouldn't be surprised if we are called upon to help bring about God's answer to it.

The tasks Jesus leaves his followers, tasks which will bring his sovereign authority to bear on the world, are straightforward enough to outline, though daunting and demanding to put into practice. The first is to *make disciples*. As Jesus called the fishermen by the sea of Galilee, and trained them up as 'learners', imitating his way of life and coming little by little to understand his kingdom message, so his followers ever since have the responsibility of calling men, women and children to follow him, and training them to understand and follow his message and his way. Evangelism – announcing God's good news, focused on Jesus, to bring people to faith and obedience – remains central to the way in which Jesus' authority is brought to bear on the world.

The second task is to *baptize* them. Baptism is not an optional extra for followers of Jesus. Jesus himself linked baptism to his own death; part of the meaning of baptism is to commit us, through plunging into water, to dying with Jesus and coming to share his new life. (Paul spells this out in Romans 6, but many other passages imply it, including the present one.) Baptism is the public, physical and visible way in which someone is marked out, branded almost, with the holy 'name'. As Jesus was given, by the angel, the name 'Jesus', signifying his real identity and the task that lay before him, so now, with his work complete, we suddenly discover that the 'name' which we are all to share is the new 'name' of the living God – the father, the son and the holy spirit.

Matthew innocently places this formula on Jesus' lips, unaware that in centuries to come it will become well known as a brilliant piece of dogmatic theology. He is, at this point, rather like someone innocently whistling a snatch of tune that a great composer will later make the centrepiece of a wonderful oratorio. Throughout the gospel he has shown us that Jesus knew himself to be, in a special sense, the unique son of the God he (and Israel as a whole) knew as 'father'. This went with his being specially equipped for his task with the 'holy spirit', the spirit who gave him the power to do what he did, and the status of being God's 'anointed' (e.g. 3.16; 12.28). Now, apparently, those who have followed Jesus and have become true disciples are themselves to be caught up in this divine life and purpose. What happened to and through Jesus in the unique gospel story is to be repeated as the message goes out into the Gentile world.

The third thing they must do is to *teach*. The gospel of Jesus generates a lifestyle quite different from the way the world lives. If Christians around the world gave as much energy to it as they do to teaching and learning so many other things, worthy in themselves but none so important as this, we would make more headway with the gospel than we usually seem to do.

But Jesus never leaves people simply with a list of commands to keep. The three instructions he has given are held in place by the promises at the beginning and end of the passage. The reason we are to do these things is because he already possesses all authority; the promise which sustains us in the task is that he is with us always and for ever. He is, as we have said, the Emmanuel. God-with-us turns into Jesus-with-us. There is no greater personal promise than that.

For reflection or discussion

- How does worship express your recognition of Jesus as the one true God who is revealed in human form? Reflect on your own worship practices and attitudes. In what ways can you cultivate a deeper sense of reverence for Jesus in your daily life?

- Consider the tasks Jesus assigns to his followers: making disciples, baptizing and teaching. Reflect on the importance of evangelism, discipleship and teaching in bringing about the authority of Jesus in the world. How can you actively engage in these tasks in your own life? What challenges or opportunities do you encounter in fulfilling these responsibilities?

Tuesday

Light out of darkness: 2 Corinthians 3.18; 4.1–6

[18]All of us, without any veil on our faces, gaze at the glory of the Lord as in a mirror, and so are being changed into the same image, from glory to glory . . .

[1]For this reason, since we have this work entrusted to us in accordance with the mercy we have received, we don't lose heart. [2]On the contrary, we have renounced the secret things that make people ashamed. We don't use tricks; we don't falsify God's word. Rather, we speak the truth openly, and recommend ourselves to everybody's conscience in the presence of God.

[3]However, if our gospel still remains 'veiled', it is veiled for people who are perishing. [4]What's happening there is that the god of this world has blinded the minds of unbelievers, so that they won't see the light of the gospel of the glory of the Messiah, who is God's image. [5]We don't proclaim ourselves, you see, but Jesus the Messiah as Lord, and ourselves as your servants because of Jesus; [6]because the God who said 'let light shine out of darkness' has shone in our hearts, to produce the light of the knowledge of the glory of God in the face of Jesus the Messiah.

I walked into the smart office, slightly early for my appointment. The porter at the front door handed me on to an assistant, who walked with me up two grand flights of stairs and through an imposing door. It was a long time since I had met the woman who was now at the head of the organization, and I wasn't even sure I would recognize her.

As we came through the door a well-dressed woman of about the right age got up and walked towards us with a smile and an out-stretched hand. Well, I thought, my memory wasn't too bad; she wasn't exactly as I remembered, but not all that far off. We shook hands. 'How very good to see you again,' I said. She looked at me with a slight surprise, and then walked back across the room to an inner door, tapped gently on it, and opened it. There, in the inner room, sat the woman I had come to see. She hadn't changed a bit. I had mistaken a personal assistant for the head of the organization.

Paul is very concerned that the Corinthians might have supposed he regarded himself as the head of the organization. He is simply a servant, a porter, a secretary, an assistant: he is merely someone who introduces people to the top man. He is one of the Messiah's office staff. Verse 5 says it all: 'We don't proclaim ourselves . . . but Jesus the Messiah as Lord.' We have to introduce people to him, not keep them in the outer office as though we ourselves were the people they should get to know. In fact, if we even began to do that we would be disloyal to our commission. Our job is to make Jesus known, and then to keep out of the way, to make sure we don't get in the light.

Because light is what this is all about. Paul may here be hinting at the moment at which, as he was filled with angry enthusiasm to persecute the young church, he was knocked to the ground by a blinding light that flashed from heaven, in which he saw the risen Jesus in all his glory. His life was transformed by that meeting, not just by the experience itself but by what he realized it meant. If Jesus was risen from the dead, he really was the Messiah. If he was the Messiah, he was the one in whom all God's purposes had come true. He was, in fact, God's son, God's image, God's new light . . .

In fact, he was the agent of God's new creation. The light that blinded Paul on the road to Damascus, the light that suddenly shone in people's hearts when he went around the world announcing the gospel of Jesus, was like the light at the very beginning, at the creation of the world. 'Let there be light,' commanded the creator God, and there was light (Genesis 1.3): a light which, as John says (John 1.5), shines in the darkness, and the darkness has not been able to put it out. With Jesus, God's new world comes into being. The gospel isn't about a different god, someone other than the world's original creator, but about the same creator God bringing new life and light to his world, the world where death and darkness have made their home and usurped his role. Paul summarizes God's command in Genesis 1, in order to say: what happened to me that day, what happened to you when you believed, and what happens whenever anyone 'turns to the Lord' (3.16), is a moment of new creation (see 5.17).

That is how Paul has come to believe that Jesus, the Messiah, is the one who reflects the living God himself. Only the living God can shine the light of new creation; and when you look at Jesus, as Paul had, face to face, you realize that you are looking at God's own glory. That gives you knowledge, knowledge of the innermost secrets of the universe, and God's saving plan for it; and in that knowledge there is more than enough light to see the way through the dark world. All of that is contained in the remarkable statement in verse 6.

This helps us to understand Paul's extraordinary confidence in verses 1 and 2. If you really believe that God has revealed himself like this in and through Jesus, and has entrusted you with the task of announcing this good news in the world, then you won't need to use the tricks of rhetoric. You won't need to play fast and loose either with the Bible itself or with the gospel message. You will simply need to speak it out, openly and unafraid. It is not, after all, a message from a god that nobody has any idea of. It is a message from the creator God, the one in whose image all human beings were made, the one of whom every human being is at least dimly aware. Everybody has a conscience to which this message will make its appeal, like a message from an almost-forgotten relative, awakening memories and hopes.

But not everybody reacts like this, as Paul himself knew only too well. Yes, he says, because the 'veil' doesn't just apply to Jewish people as he himself had been; it applies to people of all sorts. Tragically, there are many who remain blinded, 'veiled', by 'the god of this world'. That is one of Paul's ways of referring to the dark power, the satan, who opposes God's light and truth. Of course, Paul knew that, as in his own case, so in many others, the gospel could and did pierce the veil. But this is his way of making sure he doesn't fall into the trap of saying, on the one hand, that people who become Christians do so because they happen to have chosen one religious option among many, or, on the other, that the gospel of Jesus has no contact with the minds of ordinary people. It isn't so much that the gospel comes to people as a strange, alien invasion, forcing them into a mould for which they were not made. The strange, alien invasion is the one perpetrated by 'the god of this world', who stops people from seeing the healing, life-giving light of the gospel.

This passage, then, is central to Paul's view of his own job description. The Messiah is the full, true reflection of the one creator God in whose image all humans were made. To announce him is not to do something strange or outlandish, but to reveal the truth and the light that all people, however dimly, ought to recognize. Let nobody suppose that Paul is that light, or that truth. He doesn't go around talking about himself. He talks about Jesus.

For reflection or discussion

- Paul's life was radically changed by encountering the risen Jesus. How has encountering Jesus transformed your life?
- The passage speaks of Jesus as the agent of God's new creation and the embodiment of God's glory. How does that inform your perception of who Jesus is? In what ways does the light of Jesus bring newness and hope? How can you share this transformative message with others?

Wednesday

God's one and only son: Hebrews 1.1–5

¹In many ways and by many means God spoke in ancient times to our ancestors in the prophets; ²but at the end of these days he spoke to us in a son.

He appointed this son to be heir of all things;
through him, in addition, he created the worlds.
³He is the shining reflection of God's own glory,
the precise expression of his own very being;
he sustains all things through his powerful word.
He accomplished the cleansing needed for sins,

and sat down at the right of the Majesty Supreme.
⁴See how much greater he is than the angels:
the name he is granted is finer than theirs.
⁵For to which angel did God ever say, 'You are my son, today
I became your father'? Or, again, 'I will be his father, and he
will be my son'?

I once had an email from an old friend in another part of the world.
He had heard that my daughter was getting married, and in con-
gratulating me he brought me up to date on the progress of his own
daughter. Now in her teens, she had seven earrings, bright purple
hair, and rings in her lip and navel as well. He told me all this as
though seeking my sympathy for his plight, but underneath that I
heard a very different note: pride and delight. I well remembered my
friend's own teenage years: a typical rebel, with long hair, loud music,
a cigarette hanging from his lip . . . clearly his daughter was (as we
say) a chip off the old block. Looking at her, he could see his own
true self. His character – or one aspect of it, at least – was shining
out of her.

This is a cheerful and low-grade example of the sublime and exalted point which the letter to the Hebrews offers as its opening description of God and his only son. The son is 'the shining reflection
of God's own glory'; he is 'the precise expression of God's own very
being'. He is, dare we say, not just a chip off the old block – as though
there might be many such people perfectly reflecting God's own inner being – but the unique son. Look at him, and it's like looking in
a mirror at God himself. His character is exactly reproduced, plain
to see.

Actually, the word used for 'precise expression' here is the Greek
word *character*, the origin of our apparently identical English word.
But this is an interesting word in both Greek and English. When
we talk about the 'characters' in a play, and when we talk about
the 'characters' of an alphabet (the Hebrew 'characters', say, or

the Japanese), what have the two got in common? Where does the idea begin?

At the bottom of it all, in the ancient world, lies the idea of engraving, or of stamping soft or hot metal with a pattern which the metal will then continue to bear. Though the ancient world didn't have printing presses such as we have had since William Caxton in the fifteenth century, it had early equivalents that were used, particularly for making coins. The emperor would employ an engraver who carved the royal portrait, and suitable words or abbreviations, on a stamp, or die, made of hard metal. The engraver then used the stamp to make a coin, so that the coin gave the *exact impression*, or indeed expression, of what was on the stamp.

The word *character* in ancient Greek was widely used to mean just that: the accurate impression left by the stamp on the coin. From there it came to mean both the individual letters that could be produced by this method (hence the 'characters' of a language) and the 'character', in the broader sense, of a person or thing: the sort of person, the 'type' if you like (think about that word, too). And this is what our writer is saying about Jesus. It is as though the exact imprint of the father's very nature and glory has been precisely reproduced in the soft metal of the son's human nature. Now it is there for all the world to see.

Stay with the image of the emperor and his engraver a moment longer, and think about the opening two verses of this remarkable letter. Supposing the emperor had been wanting for a long time to tell his subjects who he was, to give them a good idea of his character. And supposing the metal stamp, or die, hadn't been invented yet. The emperor would only be able to send out drawings or sketches, which might tell people something but wouldn't give them the full picture. Then, at last, the reality: hard metal on soft, original picture exactly reproduced. Yes, says the writer: God has for a long time been sending advance sketches of himself to his people, but now he's given us his exact portrait.

With this idea, written as a grand and rather formal opening to the letter, the writer invites us to look at the whole sweep of biblical history and see it coming to a climax in Jesus. (Unlike the letters of Paul, this one doesn't tell us who it's from or who it's intended for, which is frustrating at one level but shouldn't spoil our enjoyment of its marvellous and rich thought.) Look back at the great prophets: Abraham, Moses, Samuel, Elijah, and then of course the writing prophets like Isaiah, Jeremiah and the rest. Our author would have included David in the list as well, as we can see from the way he quotes the Psalms.

This opening sentence isn't just a rhetorical flourish. It tells us clearly how the argument of the whole letter is going to run. Again and again we start with a passage from the Old Testament, and the writer shows us how it points forwards to something yet to come. Again and again the 'something' it points forwards to turns out to be Jesus – Jesus, as in this passage, as God's unique son, the one who has dealt with sins fully and finally, the one who now rules at God's right hand, the one to whom even angels bow in submission.

The next passage will develop this last point more fully. But we should notice, before we go any further, that the passages our writer quotes in verse 5 are two of the Old Testament passages the early Christians used most frequently when they were struggling to say what had to be said about Jesus. Psalm 2.7 and 2 Samuel 7.14 both speak of the Messiah, the ultimate son of David, as God's own special son. Like all the early Christians, the writer of this letter begins his thinking with the belief that Jesus was and is the Messiah, Israel's true king. Everything else follows from that.

For reflection or discussion

- In what ways is Jesus the 'precise expression' or 'exact imprint' of God's nature and glory? How does this revelation of Jesus as God's unique son inform your understanding of God's character and his relationship with humanity?

- Consider the significance of the imagery of engraving and stamping in relation to Jesus as the exact representation of God. What does it say about the authenticity and reliability of Jesus' revelation compared with previous 'sketches' or glimpses of God throughout biblical history?

Thursday

Jesus as the truly human being: Hebrews 2.5–9

⁵You see, God didn't place the world to come (which is what I'm writing about) under the control of angels. ⁶Someone has spoken of it somewhere in these terms:

What are humans, that you should remember them?

What is the son of man, that you should take thought for him?

⁷You made him a little lower than the angels,

you crowned him with glory and honour,

⁸and you placed everything under his feet.

When it speaks of everything being subjected to him, it leaves nothing that is not subjected to him. As things are at present, we don't see everything subjected to him. ⁹What we do see is the one who was, for a little while, made lower than the angels – that is, Jesus – crowned with glory and honour because of the suffering of death, so that by God's grace he might taste death on behalf of everyone.

One of the most dramatic stories in the Old Testament concerns the royal succession. King David was very old, and everybody knew he couldn't last much longer. He had a great many sons and daughters. One of his sons, Adonijah, got together with the head of the army and one of the senior priests and had himself proclaimed as king without David knowing. But David had promised his wife Bathsheba that her son, Solomon, would be king; so when David heard what had happened, he had Zadok the priest and Nathan the prophet anoint Solomon king instead. (You can read the whole story in the first two chapters of 1 Kings.) Everything turned on the question: who did the king intend to rule in the kingdom that was to come?

That's the question this chapter in Hebrews faces; only, instead of a kingdom to be ruled by a new king after the old one has died, it's all about the new world that is yet to be, and the way in which God intends that this coming world should be ruled. As verse 5 says, 'the world to come' is the main subject both of this passage and of the whole letter; that's why 'hope' is such a powerful theme throughout the entire book. And the thrust of a good deal of the argument is that, in Jesus the Messiah, this hope has burst into the world already, bringing sure signs of the new world that will eventually come to be.

The present passage moves through three stages to make this point. The first is that God always intended his unique son to be superior to the angels, even to the angels through whom the Jewish law had been given. This time, though, he speaks of this superiority in terms of the *future role* that has been marked out for the son. In the coming world, God intends that the original order of creation should finally be realized: the world is to be ruled, wisely and creatively, by human beings who themselves live in trusting obedience to God himself. In Genesis 1 and 2, Adam and Eve are given charge of the garden and the animals. This role, though corrupted in all sorts of ways through the 'fall' in Genesis 3, is reaffirmed in Psalm 8, from which Hebrews now quotes. What are human beings? asks the psalm. Why does God treat them in such a special way, when they are so obviously small and insignificant in terms of the wider creation? The answer is mysterious and powerful: humans seem at the moment to be lower than the angels, a lesser order of beings, but God intends that they should become the world's true governors. That's what being 'crowned with glory and honour' means.

The passage, though, has an extra twist. The word for 'humans' in verse 6 is singular, 'a human being'. In the next line, the phrase 'son of man', which to a Jewish reader could simply mean 'a typical human being', could also, to someone who knew either the book of Daniel or the teaching of Jesus, mean 'the Messiah' – highlighting the fact that the Messiah is now to be seen as the true, typical, authentic and representative human being. This is what Hebrews has in mind, as we can see from the way in which the last line of the quotation, about God placing everything under his feet, picks up the passage from Psalm 110 quoted in 1.13 ('sit at my right hand, until I make your enemies a stool for your feet'). Just like Paul in 1 Corinthians 15.20–28, Hebrews brings together these texts about the Messiah and about the truly human one in order to speak both of the *future* role of Jesus in God's new creation and of his *present* position, already exalted as Lord. The point Hebrews adds is that, according to Psalm 8, this means that the Messiah is superior to the angels. This important part of his argument is now complete.

The second stage of this passage is the reflection on how Jesus has already attained the status which God marked out for humans in general. The psalm speaks of humankind in general as set in authority over the world, with 'everything subjected to him'. But, says Hebrews, this clearly hasn't happened yet. Humans are not ruling the world, bringing God's order and justice to bear on the whole of creation. Everything is still in a state of semi-chaos. How then can this psalm be taken seriously?

The answer is that it *has* happened – in the case of Jesus. He is the representative of the human race. His exaltation as Lord after his earthly ministry, suffering and death (in which he was indeed 'lower than the angels') has placed him in the role marked out from the beginning for the human race. He has gone ahead of the rest of us into God's future, the future in which order and justice – saving order, healing justice – will come to the world.

But how can something that's happened to Jesus, all by himself, be relevant for the rest of us? This brings us to the third stage of the passage. Jesus is the *representative* of his people. In a parliamentary democracy, voters in each area elect someone to *represent* them in the central councils of state. They can't all be there themselves so they find an appropriate way of appointing someone who is there *on their behalf*, carrying their hopes and fears, their needs and aspirations, in his or her own person. Thus, because the representative is there and they are not, he or she also acts as their *substitute*, doing for them what, for various reasons, they can't do for themselves.

Something like this is going on again and again in the New Testament when writers speak of Jesus both as Israel's Messiah and the world's true Lord. Jesus *represents* Israel, as its Messiah; and, since Israel was designed, in God's purpose, to be the people who would represent the whole world, he also represents that much larger community. As a result, he can stand in for them, doing for them what they can't do for themselves.

Hebrews here puts it in a nutshell: in his suffering of death, Jesus has, by God's grace, been enabled 'to taste death on behalf of everyone'. A good deal of the letter is devoted to explaining how this comes about, and what it means. For the moment, we should simply celebrate the fact, which is central to all Christianity, that in Jesus God has already dealt with death on our behalf, and is already ruling the world as its rightful Lord.

For reflection or discussion

- Consider the tension between the present state of the world, characterized by chaos and the absence of God's perfect order, and the future reality envisioned in Psalm 8 and fulfilled in Jesus. How does the exaltation of Jesus as Lord give you hope for the ultimate restoration of order and justice in creation?
- Reflect on the connections between Jesus' earthly ministry, his suffering and his exaltation as Lord. How does this understanding

deepen your appreciation for Jesus' unique role in bridging the gap between God and humanity?

Friday

Jesus revealed: Revelation 1.9–20

[9]I, John, your brother and your partner in the suffering, the kingdom, and the patient endurance in Jesus, was on the island called Patmos because of the word of God and the testimony of Jesus. [10]I was in the spirit on the Lord's day, and I heard behind me a loud voice like a trumpet. [11]'Write down what you see in a book,' it said, 'and send it to the seven churches: to Ephesus, Smyrna, Pergamum, Thyatira, Sardis, Philadelphia and Laodicea.'

[12]So I turned to see the voice that was speaking with me. As I turned, I saw seven golden lampstands, [13]and in the middle of the lampstands 'one like a son of man', wearing a full-length robe and with a golden belt across his chest. [14]His head and his hair were white, white like wool, white like snow. His eyes were like a flame of fire, [15]his feet were like exquisite brass, refined in a furnace, and his voice was like the sound of many waters. [16]He was holding seven stars in his right hand, and a sharp two-edged sword was coming out of his mouth. The sight of him was like the sun when it shines with full power. [17]When I saw him, I fell at his feet as though I was dead.

He touched me with his right hand. 'Don't be afraid,' he said. 'I am the first and the last [18]and the living one. I was dead, and look! I am alive for ever and ever. I have the keys of death and Hades. [19]Now write what you see, both the things that already are, and also the things that are going to happen subsequently. [20]The secret meaning of the seven stars which you saw in my right hand, by the way, and the seven golden lampstands, is this. The seven stars are the angels of the seven churches, and the seven lampstands are the seven churches themselves.

Some years ago there was an eclipse of the sun. This happens rarely enough, and to witness it is a great experience. But staring at the sun, as it slips behind the moon and then emerges the other side, is dangerous. If you look through binoculars, or a telescope, the sun's power on your eye can do permanent damage. It can even cause blindness.

On this particular occasion, there were public warnings broadcast on radio and television, and printed in the newspapers, to the effect that people should be careful. Only look, they said, through special dark glasses. Eventually one person, who obviously had very little understanding of natural phenomena, got cross about all this. Surely, they thought, this was a 'health and safety' issue. A letter was sent to the London *Times*: if this event was so dangerous, why were the government allowing it in the first place?

Fortunately, even the most totalitarian of governments has not yet been able to control what the sun and the moon get up to. But the danger of full-power sunlight is worth contemplating as we hear John speaking about his vision of Jesus. As I write this, the sun has just emerged through watery clouds; even so, I can't look at it for more than a second before having to turn away. So when John, with the brightness of a Mediterranean sky in his mind, speaks of Jesus in this way (verse 16), we should learn to think of this Jesus with a new kind of reverence.

For some, Jesus is just a faraway figure of first-century fantasy. For others, including some of today's enthusiastic Christians, Jesus is the one with whom we can establish a personal relationship of loving intimacy. John would agree with the second of these, but he would warn against imagining that Jesus is therefore a cosy figure, one who merely makes us feel happy inside. To see Jesus as he is would drive us not to snuggle up to him, but to fall at his feet as though we were dead.

Jesus revealed

This vision of Jesus (verses 12–16) introduces us to several things about the way John writes. Like someone reporting a strange dream, the things he says are hard to imagine all together. It's more like looking at a surrealist painting, or a set of shifting computer-generated images. It's not a simple sketch. For a start, when John hears a voice like a trumpet (verse 10), he tells us that he 'turned to see the voice'. There is a sense in which this is just right: the Jesus whom he then sees is indeed the Voice, the living Word of the father, the one through whom God spoke and still speaks. And the words which Jesus himself speaks turn into a visible sword coming out of his mouth (verse 16), echoing Isaiah's prophecy both about the coming king (11.4) and about the suffering servant (49.2).

In particular, this vision of Jesus draws together the two characters in one of the most famous biblical visions, that of Daniel 7. There, as the suffering of God's people reaches its height, 'the Ancient of Days' takes his seat in heaven, and 'one like a son of man' (in other words, a human figure, representing God's people and, in a measure, all the human race) is presented before him, and enthroned alongside him. Now, in John's vision, these two pictures seem to have merged. When we are looking at Jesus, he is saying, we are looking straight through him at the father himself.

Hold the picture in your mind, detail by detail. Let those eyes of flame search you in and out. Imagine standing beside a huge waterfall, its noise like sustained thunder, and imagine that noise as a human voice, echoing round the hills and round your head. And then imagine his hand reaching out to touch you . . .

Yes, fear is the natural reaction. But here, as so often, Jesus says, 'Don't be afraid.' It's all right. Yes, you are suffering, and your people are suffering (verse 9). Yes, the times are strange and hard, with harsh and severe rulers running the world and imposing their will on city after city. But the seven churches – seven is the number of perfection, and the churches listed in verse 11 thus stand for all churches in the world, all places and all times – need to know that Jesus himself is

173

standing in their midst, and that the 'angels' who represent and look after each of them are held in his right hand.

And the Jesus in question has as his credentials the fact that he 'was dead', and is 'alive for ever' (verse 18). Like someone whispering to us that they know the secret way out of the dungeon where we have been imprisoned, he says, 'I've got the keys! The keys of death and Hades – I have them right here! There's nothing more you need worry about.'

For reflection or discussion

- What is the nature of your relationship with Jesus? Do you primarily see him as a comfortable and cosy figure, or are you open to encountering him as an awe-inspiring and transformative presence? How can a balanced view of Jesus as both intimate and awe-inspiring deepen your faith and relationship with him?
- How does the knowledge that Jesus holds the keys to death and Hades bring comfort and assurance? How can this truth transform your perspective on suffering, fear and the challenges of life?

Saturday

The Word made flesh: John 1.1–18

[1]In the beginning was the Word. The Word was close beside God, and the Word was God. [2]In the beginning, he was close beside God.

[3]All things came into existence through him; not one thing that exists came into existence without him. [4]Life was in him, and this life was the light of the human race. [5]The light shines in the darkness, and the darkness did not overcome it.

[6]There was a man called John, who was sent from God. [7]He came as evidence, to give evidence about the light, so that

everyone might believe through him. [8]He was not himself the light, but he came to give evidence about the light.

[9]The true light, which gives light to every human being, was coming into the world. [10]He was in the world, and the world was made through him, and the world did not know him. [11]He came to what was his own, and his own people did not accept him. [12]But to anyone who did accept him, he gave the right to become God's children; yes, to anyone who believed in his name. [13]They were not born from blood, or from fleshly desire, or from the intention of a man, but from God.

[14]And the Word became flesh, and lived among us. We gazed upon his glory, glory like that of the father's only son, full of grace and truth.

[15]John gave evidence about him, loud and clear.

'This is the one', he said, 'that I was speaking about when I told you, "The one who comes after me ranks ahead of me, because he was before me."'

[16]Yes; it's out of his fullness that we have all received, grace indeed on top of grace. [17]The law, you see, was given through Moses; grace and truth came through Jesus the Messiah. [18]Nobody has ever seen God. The only-begotten God, who is intimately close to the father – he has brought him to light.

'In the beginning' – no Bible reader could see that phrase and not think at once of the start of Genesis, the first book in the Old Testament: 'In the beginning God created the heavens and the earth.' Whatever else John is going to tell us, he wants us to see how the creator God is acting in a new way within his much-loved creation – how the long story which began in Genesis reaches the climax the creator had always intended.

And John does this through telling us about 'the Word'. In Genesis 1, the climax is the creation of humans, made in God's image. In John 1, it is the arrival of a human being, the Word become 'flesh'.

When I speak a word, it is, in a sense, part of me. It's a breath that comes from inside me, making the noise that I give it with my throat, my mouth and my tongue. When people hear it, they assume I intended it. 'But you said . . .' people comment, if our deeds don't match up to our words. We remain responsible for the words we say.

And yet our words have a life which seems independent of us. When people hear them, words can change the way they think and live. Think of 'I love you'; or 'It's time to go'; or 'You're fired'. These words create new situations. People respond or act accordingly. The words remain in their memory and go on affecting them.

In the Old Testament, God regularly acts by means of his 'word'. What he says, happens – in Genesis itself, and regularly thereafter. 'By the word of the Lord', says the psalm, 'the heavens were made' (33.6). God's word is the one thing that will last, even though people and plants wither and die (Isaiah 40.6–8); God's word will go out of his mouth and bring life, healing and hope to Israel and the whole creation (Isaiah 55.10–11). That's part of what lies behind John's choice of 'Word' here, as a way of telling us who Jesus really is.

John probably expects some readers to see that this opening passage says, about Jesus himself, what some writers had said about 'Wisdom'. Many Jewish teachers had grappled with the age-old questions: How can the one true God be both different from the world and active within the world? How can he be remote, holy and detached, and also intimately present? Some had already spoken of the 'word' and 'wisdom' as ways of answering these questions. Some had already combined them within the belief that the one true God had promised to place his own 'presence' within the Temple in Jerusalem. Others saw them enshrined in the Jewish law, the Torah. All of this is present in John's mind when he writes of God's 'Word'.

But the idea of the Word would also make some of his readers think of ideas that pagan philosophers had discussed. Some spoke of the 'word' as a kind of principle of rationality, lying deep within the whole cosmos and within all human beings. Get in touch with this principle, they said, and your life will find its true meaning. Well, maybe, John is saying to them; but the Word isn't an abstract principle, it's a person. And I'm going to introduce you to him.

Verses 1–2 and 18 begin and end the passage by stressing that the Word was and is God, and is intimately close to God. John knows perfectly well he's making language go beyond what's normally possible, but it's Jesus that makes him do it; because verse 14 says that the Word became flesh – that is, became human, became one of us. He became, in fact, the human being we know as Jesus. If you want to know who the true God is, look long and hard at Jesus.

The rest of the passage clusters around this central statement. The one we know as Jesus is identical, it seems, with the Word who was there from the very start, the Word through whom all things were made, the one who contained and contains life and light. The Word challenged the darkness before creation and now challenges the darkness that is found, tragically, within creation itself. The Word is bringing into being the new creation, in which God says once more, 'Let there be light!'

Perhaps the most exciting thing about this opening passage is that we're in it too: 'To anyone who did accept him' (verse 12) – that means anyone at all, then and now. You don't have to be born into a particular family or part of the world. God wants people from everywhere to be born in a new way, born into the family which he began through Jesus and which has since spread through the world. Anyone can become a 'child of God' in this sense, a sense which goes beyond the fact that all humans are special in God's sight. Something can happen to people in this life which causes them to become new people, people who (as verse 12 says) 'believe in his name'.

Somehow the great drama of God and the world, of Jesus and Israel, of the Word who reveals the glory of the unseen God – this great drama is a play in search of actors, and there are parts for everyone, you and me included.

For reflection or discussion

- Consider the power and influence of words in our lives. Reflect on the significance of God's word as a creative force and a means of communication. How does recognizing the impact of God's word in the Old Testament inform your understanding of Jesus as the Word in the New Testament?
- Reflect on your role in God's drama of redemption. How can you actively participate in the story that God is telling?

N. T. Wright is Research Professor Emeritus of New Testament and Early Christianity at the University of St Andrews, Scotland, and Senior Research Fellow at Wycliffe Hall, Oxford. He is the author of numerous books, including the New Testament for Everyone series, *Every Day for Everyone: 365 Devotions from Genesis to Revelation* (with John Goldingay) and *What Did the Cross Accomplish? A Conversation about the Atonement* (with Simon Gathercole and Robert B. Stewart).